Sabreta,
Dear one, I pray this
story of redemption fills
you with the hope of the
Healer. *& Your sister is amazing &*
I thank God for her!
Shannyn Caldwell

THE HEALING
SEASON

HOW A DEADLY TORNADO NEARLY DESTROYED AND COMPLETLY RESHAPED MY FAITH

D1362366

Shannyn Caldwell

for mom and dad

CONTENTS

A WORD OF THANKS

Before I began to write this book, I went to my husband, Joseph. I asked him what boundaries he wanted to put up as I began to tell our not always pretty story. His answer? Tell the truth. Tell the truth and make sure God is glorified. With those two simple instructions, I had the freedom to bring you this book. So, to Joseph Caldwell, thank you. What a blessing it is to walk this walk with you. Thank you for delivering my note.

Then, I went to my brother, Ryan Cook and asked him the same question: what boundaries into the underpinnings of our family would *he* would like to see? His answer was a near mirror of Joseph's. "Give God glory," he said, "aside from that, just tell the truth." Thanks Buddy. Thank you for praying for me all those years I didn't know Him. Thanks to your beautiful family. I love you.

Thanks to my kids for living through this experience with such unwavering faith in God and in me. Thanks for trusting me during those times I said, "I know it looks bad, but God's gonna do something good." Thank you for believing and for encouraging me, for rooting me on and for praying. Grandpa Lee and Grandma Jacque would have loved you so much. I pray that in some way, you can get to know them better from what is written here. Alexandra and Liam, I thank God for you and love you to infinity and beyond.

To the people who showed up when we were crashing and burning (many of whom are depicted in these pages and many others were serving alongside those named here) thank you for your comfort, love, support and discipleship us; especially Jim and Megan Pool of the Renaissance Vineyard Church in Ferndale, Michigan. Wow, you guys, think of where we'd be today if you would not have given me that black leather Bible, then followed up. Thank you.

Thank you to the army of people whose finger prints are all over this book. Thanks to Nancy Rue. Lady, it was your mentorship that brought this from a blog to a book. You helped bring Mom and Dad back to life in these pages and I can never thank you enough.

This book is beautiful on the *outside*, not just the inside, and that's because of Joy McMillian, who also happens to be beautiful inside and out. The cover is my dream cover. Thank you! Todd Davis thanks for your skillful editing and for being one of the most generous brainstormers on the planet and to Scott Rutherford for taking his red pen to the project at the finish line.

Thanks to Shanna Gregor and to the Family Life Radio team for their prayers, encouragement, wisdom and support. Thanks, Dawn Heitger for being such an impeccable introduction into the world to Christian radio. You inspired me then. You inspire me now. Your example calls me to excellence.

Peter Brooks, thanks for walking the walk and for having a pun for everything.

To the friends, family and listeners who have prayed this book up – thank you!

Thanks to the American Red Cross.

Thanks to the One went to the cross so we could be healed.

FORWARD

The Healing Season is a story of Christ's intentional love breaking through into the life of one hurting woman. It epitomizes the reality of what can happen when a person looks beyond their personal hurt into the eyes of a loving Father. On every page Shannyn Caldwell opens the secret places of her life, drawing you into the deeper truth that God's love for her is available to each of us. This is a great read for anyone who desires more from life than just getting by or getting through, and is searching for the true source of healing.

Dr. Randy Carlson New York Times Best Selling Author, President of Family Life Communications and Host of Intentional Living.

CHAPTER 1

WHAT *IS* THE HEALING SEASON?

"I did the math. The anniversary of the tornado is April 9th. Today is March 30th and the Lord healed my heart 10 days ago. That means for 3,996 days, I lived with an utterly blown-up, exploded, pulverized mess of a broken heart. If you include the fact that it was already broken at the time the tornado that killed both my parents hit, I was a broken and beat up mess for 4,511 days, and as of now, I've been healed for 10."

This was a personal journal entry 10 days into a 40-day promise I made to a dear friend – my pastor, Jim Pool. It was a promise I made *to* him, but *for* myself, and for my husband Joseph and our kids. I was used to being broken. I was over it. I accepted it, but it was hurting my family. For that reason, I made a promise to journal daily. To journal like my life depended on it – because frankly, as you will see from the excerpts from the journal at the top of each chapter, it did. It was a promise I made to *myself*, too, because I knew I was still sinking – all these years later, still gasping for air. I was holding on for dear life, but I didn't think of my life as all that *dear*.

1

D on't get me wrong. I loved my husband, my children, the garden outside, but not enough to actually love living my life. I'll give you an analogy from my childhood. If you're squeamish, skip this next part. When I was nine years old I was playing at my friend, Beth Burton's house. She lived at the top of the big hill by our school. For fun, we'd put on our roller skates and go all the way down the hill, cut a hard right at the bottom, zip into the tennis court by the playground and spin around. We felt like *Dorothy Hamill All Stars* with *Charlie's Angels* hair. The last time I tried it, I went flying down the hill, cut a hard right into the tennis court as usual, but that time, as I started my spin, some gravel got stuck in my wheels and I landed hard on my right knee. The concrete court tore straight through my blue jeans, my skin and ME!

This will be the hard part for you weak stomach types. It. Was. Gaping. To this day, I'm truly surprised my kneecap's still connected. It was gushing at first and required a compress and then gauze, which Beth's mom, a nurse, expertly administered. It was bandaged for days. "What a rip-off!" I remember thinking. At least I could have gotten a real *cast* out of the deal! When I could finally remove the gauze for good, there was a giant – and I mean *covered-my-whole- kneecap-big* scab that was shaped like the continent of Africa. I remember my mom and dad jokingly called it my "Africa scab."

My Africa scab stayed there for a really long time – at least a month. Occasionally, curiosity would get the best of me, or maybe it was simple impatience. Unable to believe that I was still not healed, I'd pull up the edges of it to see what it looked like under there and every time, it was clear this was not healed. There was still just a gaping wound with a scab on top (Squeamish stomach alert lifted).

That's how I felt when my wise friend and I agreed to this 40-day promise. This season. This journal. I thought I was healed up enough to "do" my life, walk around and interact with others. But not to live – really *live*– my life. Maybe you've felt that way.

I was "the walking wounded."

This may surprise you, but by the time I made this promise to embark upon my healing season, I was already saved (that's Christianese for someone who has accepted Jesus Christ as their Savior). In fact, Pastor Jim and his wife, Megan had given me my first Bible. They introduced me to Jesus years before and told me about His promises and His healing power. I believed them and still do. I am a believer – that's also Christianese for someone who has accepted Jesus as Savior – so let's just get that out in the open right away. This book is my story of healing, and the Healer is Jesus. I don't want you to feel like you've been given a bait and switch. The deal is this: Jesus healed me from the loss of both parents in a tornado, from divorce and from a turbulent remarriage. I want to share with you the story of how He did it, because Jesus didn't wave a magic wand. I went to Him for healing – and He healed. So, if you are in need of healing today, you are in the right place. Even if you do not follow Jesus, let me tell you what He did for me and you can decide for yourself. I was a total mess and He healed me. Most importantly, if He did it for me, *He can do it for you.* When I first accepted Christ, I thought there *would* be a magic wand moment and I would see radical, total healing in every part of my life. My marriage – perfect! My emotional turmoil – calmed. Parenting problems – resolved. Finances – in order. I thought that maybe, just maybe, everything would instantly get better, just like in *The Wizard of Oz* when the picture goes from drab sepia tones to glorious Technicolor.

It didn't.

OK, yes, I knew where I was going when I died, which was something I stressed about on a daily basis before I met Jesus. I no longer felt the need to be anxious about that feeling that constantly nagged me as I lived the life of someone who believed they had to earn their way to Heaven. Had I been good enough? Had I done enough to make it in? That worry was lifted. I knew where I was going. Because of Jesus, I was going to heaven when I died and nothing could change that – not even messed-up me.

I now had a playbook for my life. I had the Bible and now I knew what to do in any given situation: Open the Bible, see what it says and then do it.

Yet I was still bitter, overly sensitive, paranoid, less than 100% available to my husband and kids. I was a chronic eye-roller. I was short-tempered, always on defense. Always looking around the corner for the next loss – the next blow to my gut. I spent too much time on my hair, too little time on my home. My laundry was never done and I resented that. I didn't trust anyone, especially myself.

I was a mess. I was my Africa scab: All grown up but nothing more than a crusty oozing mess with cutie hair and a manicure. I looked almost-healed on the surface, but when you pulled up my edges, I was still bleeding and it was just as hard to live with as that bulky bandage. I had tried anything and everything to fill in that space, that brokenness, that longing to be known, wanted and loved and at peace. I tried long walks with my husband, which often resulted not in hand holding, but practically in street fights. I tried long walks with my dog, which still left me picking up a mess. I tried gardening. I tried aromatherapy, talk therapy, hydrotherapy and hypnosis. I tried boxing. I tried meditation. I did thousands of hours of yoga. I did weekend workshops on grief and recovery. But no matter how many zillions of times I focused on statements like "I trust the process of life," I didn't. I did not trust the process. I did not trust life. I did not trust: not my husband, not myself, not anyone. I loved. I did not trust. I lived on edge, in constant fear and worry. I could not integrate back into my life. It was then that my counselor suggested a prescription for anti-depressants – which I rejected.

"They make everyone I know fat," I said.

I was stuck. I was out of options. My friends were exhausted and moving on with their lives. And I was 100% at a loss. I couldn't live joyfully in my own life and I couldn't die, though there were times when I wished I could.

Mother's Day was the worst day of the year for me back then. The one thing that brought some peace to that storm was a tradition that stayed with us a long time because it did somehow bring stillness in the chaos. Even the *thought* of Mother's Day without my mom was like being in a torture chamber. Anyone of any age who has lost their mom understands that. It was Laura, my counselor, who suggested a simple way to remember Mom on Mother's Day. She said I should get a helium balloon and attach a note to my mother on it and then let it go! She said that it might also be helpful for my daughter, who was three at the time. And so we sent our first awkward attempt sailing skyward and the tradition stuck. Seeing the balloon go up, up and away would help Alex understand that just as we can't see the balloon any longer, but we know it's still there somewhere, so it is with Grandma and Grandpa.

We did it on Mother's Day at noon Eastern Time every year.

My brother, Ryan, who lived in Dayton with his Young Life leader, would also get a balloon and we talked on cell-phones while grasping tight to the curling ribbon and count down through tears – three-two-one – as we let our crinkly silver love offerings soar higher and higher and then disappear.

"See Alex," I said. "It's like that with Grandma and Grandpa. They're still out there somewhere. We just can't see them. We have to let them go."

We did that for years. Alexandra and I even have framed Mom and Daughter pictures from the years of letting the balloons go. It became a fun adventure for us, trying to outdo ourselves each year with progressively more amazing balloons. One year we got a giant laminate balloon from a flower shop. It was spaceship-huge and shaped like an entire pot of sunflowers. The next year it was a yellow rose-shaped affair. Daddy used to always get Mom yellow roses. We had reached the ultimate in balloon-choosing and Mom would have loved it.

I wish I could say I loved it, too. Part of me did. But part of me felt like it was just more denial. Just a way to ignore all the other people who got to go to brunch with their moms and give them real corsages pinned to lacy perfumed dresses. We carried on with the

Mother's Day balloons until my brother called one year and shared that he didn't really want to "do the balloon thing this year" as it "kinda bummed him out." And I got that. I felt that way too. It was never going to replace her. It was just getting sad. I wonder, though, when I get to heaven, if Mom will have a collection of deflated balloons and love notes from her babies. I guess we did it until we were ready to let go of the tradition, just like the balloon. I think, though, there are some things we can't just let go. There are some we want to let go of, yet cannot seem to on our own. These are the things we cling to.

I'm not convinced that it's even necessarily a conscious choice, this clinging. I think it may be built in.

Factory installed.

Standard equipment.

Creatures of habit.

This urge to remain and to remain the same.

Like the way we make the same foods at Christmas, drive home the same way each day.

The way "Pooh Bear" must have honey – even though he really *could* eat other things. Like the way that Duggar mom gets a makeover and comes out with the same exact hair. Our habits have a way of becoming who we are, and I was very much in the habit of having a mom and dad. I was still having severe withdrawal years later.

Even after I accepted Christ, which I'll explain more later, I continued searching for anything that would take the pain away. Before you ask the obvious question, yes, I did bring it to God and ask Him to heal me. I asked thousands of times. In fact, I felt like He *had* healed me on several occasions, but within days – or minutes even – the same old mess would come back up. It didn't stick. It didn't stay. If you've ever felt that feeling, hang on. There's hope.

The two things that kept me sane in my pre-saved days were the same things that keep many unsaved people from totally crashing: Counseling therapy and my weekly yoga class.

After God removed the scales from my eyes by showing me the meaning of the cross of Christ and I accepted Him wholeheartedly as my Savior, I continued to practice yoga and still do. I understand that Jesus has taken everything into His authority. There is nothing that does not belong to Him and that has not been reconciled by Him. I'm completely covered in Christ. I practice without any fear whatsoever. It is worship for me now – but it was then, too. In the quiet of my breath, I could finally find some comfort. My teachers were so kind and the music so gentle. They used words like "good" and "let go" and "relax into it." Who talks to you like that, anyway – all gentle and kind? Moms of infants and yoga teachers. End of list. I needed that. I needed to hear someone say kind and lovely things and tell me to keep breathing.

I needed it because life at home was, frankly, still hard, even though I was saved. Joseph and I did not know *how* to be married. Neither of us was saved when we began dating or married life, and we had no idea how to practice sacrificial love. We were devastating to one another. I craved kindness. I needed someone to tell me I was doing well and that this growing and healing was a process. Yoga class filled that need for tenderness. And with all that sweetness for an hour of class and all that deep breathing, I'd think, *Eureka! I've found it! My happy place! Here it IS! Hold onto this feeling!* Then, half an hour later I'd be at the grocery store check-out acting out aggression. I'd be like: "Really lady? The sign says 15 items or less. You've got like, 16, 17 items in there. Where's the manager?"

It wasn't deep peace. It wasn't lasting. It was like a good blow-out at the beauty shop: Eventually the wind whips up or some water flies by and there goes the neighborhood.

I'd gotten more than a blow-out, though. My divorce blew me up, but I was able to recover. The tornado blew me *up* and I was *not* able to recover. My new husband and kids had a wreck on their hands. I had no idea what it was like to just "be," let alone, to be still – to find inner peace.

One night, after a long day of fending off bill collectors and taking care of our nine-month old, I escaped to the quiet solace of the yoga studio to practice. It was a particularly challenging class that night, but I loved and trusted my teacher so completely that I was willing to try things which really scared me.

"Sit quietly and focus on your breath," she said in her gentle voice. "Draw your shoulder blades onto your back and feel your heart open."

Feel my heart *open*? I don't think so. I've tried that before. It was ugly.

She slowly continued, "Just soften. Open. Open to grace."

I decided to try it, one more time. I would open. I would soften. I felt my heart open like a flower and shine like the sun. I felt… alive, and for the first time in a long while, I was grateful. I inhaled and exhaled my way through an hour of postures. Warrior: I am strong. Mountain: I am stable. Child: I am vulnerable. Dancer: I am full of grace. Final resting pose: I am letting go.

I drove home feeling like the most lovely, confident woman in the universe. I was sure that it was just a matter of time before I was healed. At the moment, I wasn't just feeling peaceful, I was feeling bliss! Then, I got home.

"What did you do all day?" Joe said the moment my foot hit the doorway "Cuz you sure didn't clean this house!"

And my perfect peace that I had so skillfully and bravely cultivated crashed down on me like my first attempt at a handstand. I fell. I fell hard.

My response: "What do you mean? I cleaned today. The house is fine."

"Well it sure doesn't look like you cleaned. It needs a touch up and YOU could use a touch up, too."

My newly opened heart, the one I had just taken the risk to expose, was pulled out of my chest and stomped to a pulp on my dirty hardwood floors.

"Joe! What do you WANT FROM ME?" I shouted through tears. "YOU clean the house if it bugs you! OTHER people think the house is fine. OTHER people think I'm BEAUTIFUL!"

"WHAT other people? No one I know. Everyone I know thinks you're stuck up. You know that, right? That everyone thinks you're a snob?"

"And everyone thinks YOU'RE a jerk and you know WHY? Because you ARE," I shouted like a siren. Now mind you, I was *saved* at this point. I was born again and yet my newly created self was still fearful, bitter, grieving and lashing out. I didn't know God's Word at that point, not well enough to live it out. I knew, "protect yourself." I knew, "fight." I knew Jesus, but I didn't know how to submit to His authority, let alone the authority of my husband. I knew broken.

"This is a joke," Joe said.

"I can't do this," I said, still crying.

"I CAN, but I don't want to," he said.

I remembered my ex-husband's extra fast and super permanent exit.

The thoughts collided in my head. *He can't leave. He can't leave. I can't leave.* But I knew he could and I thought for sure he would.

"We need help," I said.

He snapped back, "You got THAT right, sister."

I took that as agreement and called our friends Jim and Meg. Now, Meg had given me my first Bible and, as I mentioned, Jim was our pastor. They are two of the kindest, most honest people on the planet. They were the first Christians I'd ever met who seemed real. Normal. If you invited them to the party, they'd come! Meg had a braid down her back and wore hippie skirts. Jim usually preached barefoot and in khaki shorts. They were like us... but, not. They knew how to fight and win. Not fight and lose it all.

They were happy – really, truly happy – to have us over to talk about our troubles. But it wasn't our marriage that we ended up talking to Jim and Meg about that night. It was my breakdown. The one I'd had the night before.

I was at a friend's house for a "Mom's Night In." It was in late March and we were all so grateful to see the snow start melting. We'd been closed up in thick socks and rubber boots for months and all of us Detroiters were in desperate need of some warmth. We spent the evening eating olives, chocolate and cheese, toasting the arrival of spring. We all had the hope that we would indeed live to see another thaw. We laughed and noshed on truffles as our shoulders unwrapped from around our ears. It was truly a great night and then, just as we were all giving our hugs and saying our good nights, the hostess mentioned how tired she was of her mom being around now that they were living together and how she wished that she could have just a little tiny break from her.

Now, anyone could understand that, right? She was beat! She'd just hosted a party and wanted quiet time. No matter how much we love our parents, as adults we don't always want them around. If most of us were honest, as much as we may love our folks we don't really want to LIVE with them. Not every minute of every day, right? Right.

Wrong. My reaction could best be classified as allergic. I lost it on my poor sweet sister-friend and her dear husband who re-surfaced as the hen once the party was finally over. My response was a tearful, "Well at least you have your mother. I'm all alone," and I proceeded to sob and sob and sob. It was ridiculous. If I had been wearing fake lashes, I would have cried them straight *off*. I couldn't stop. I knew it wasn't rational, but I could not stop. And I was scared.

We went to talk to Jim and Meg about our marriage the next night, but Joseph's and my problems could only be as healed as we were healed. As he was healed, as I was healed…and we both had a long, long way to go.

I repentantly unveiled the embarrassment of the night before. The scene hadn't ended when I got home, and Joseph explained how much the problem-solving man in him was undone by his constantly weeping bride. I think his exact words were, "I can't stand it. It hurts me. It hurts our family. I can't fix it. I can't fix her."

When Pastor Jim asked about my therapy and if medication may be a good solution for a time, I again expressed my lack of desire to be medicated saying, "I don't want to be drugged. I want to be healed. Jesus is the healer, right?"

"What helps, Shannyn?" Pastor Jim asked. "Anything? You're a writer, right? Are you still writing? Does it help?"

"Yes," I said. "It helps in the moment."

"Anything else help? Prayer? Does prayer help?"

"Yes. Prayer helps a lot."

"OK. I have an idea. How about this, you freak out every day, right?"

I nodded.

"And is it triggered by the snow melting?"

I nodded again and added, "When it turns to spring." I feel tears start to well up. "See?"

"And when does it pass…move out?"

"Mother's Day," I said and I started to sob, reaching across them to the Kleenex on the end table.

"OK, then every day from now till Mother's Day…that's… 40 days," he said, checking the calendar on his phone. "I want you to write. Whenever you start to feel it coming on, sit down and write. Write until you feel normal or at least normal-ish again. And get prayer with a partner twice every week. Every single Wednesday at house group and every single Sunday after church, I want you to grab someone and have them pray for you specifically for this hurting and brokenness. Even if you feel OK, write every day, and get prayer every single time, OK?"

Fine.

For 40 days, I could do it. The hard season, the time from winter's thaw to Mother's Day would become my healing season. Why not?

So the next day I began . . .

I promised I'd journal because my brokenness is affecting other people, not just me.

I don't want to.

It hurts

It hurts to write about the things I need to write about.

It hurts to remember the smell of the broken trees mixed with the smell of chainsaw and my mother's best coat covered in mud.

My breath is short.

Besides, I'd written it all down already. Repeatedly. I'd written the order of events and how I was feeling when they died. I thought, "How many times do I have to do this?" It wasn't going to bring them back. It wasn't one of those things you could look at and say, "Well, it can't hurt." It could hurt. And it did.

But I was hurting anyway, so I looked at the challenge and decided to dig in deeper one more time and fight. I would fight for my marriage, for my peace and for my healing. I would take another risk and try to trust again. I would open my heart and my life again. I had to. I had no other choice, or I was going to lose my husband and every last bit of hope I had in this life. I would do it. I had to do it.

Who would have guessed from that beginning that just 10 days in, I would discover a hidden treasure? Like the pearl of great price, hidden right there in plain sight, right where I'd buried it. I've learned, by God's grace, to embrace life's treasure with open hands and to let go of so much more than that balloon on Mother's Day. In fact, I've realized that it was never about the balloon in the first place. It was always about the letting go – watching the things we've loved just fly away and resisting the urge to launch ourselves from the ground and flail through the air chasing after them, when they are not for us to grasp. It is, as the Bible says, "to inherit the wind."

So I stand, hands still open, not only to continue my own journey – which is far from over – but to reach out to my fellow journeymen and women who still hold on to the past with both hands, their teeth, and whatever else they can use to keep the pain in and the horror out.

We all have tornados. We all suffer loss. But we don't have to suffer forever.

What I want to do is tell my story, as I remember it. I'll share my prayers through my healing journal pages at the beginning of each chapter. I'll share my brokenness so you see you don't need to have it together to get it together. And more importantly, I want to share my healing. And as I tell and share, I want to try to explain the insights God has shown me in this journey, things that I know can be helpful to anyone – from the grieving Sandy Hook parent to the numbed victim of sexual abuse. From the neglected child to the recovering war veteran, I want to bring you along on this path with me, talk to you about the healing you don't even think is possible, either for yourself or someone you know who is struggling toward the breaking point.

You may be thinking, just like I did, that no one can understand your story, your pain.

That is, in part, very true. I don't and can't truly know what you've gone through and perhaps are still going through. In many ways, I can barely understand my own story. We are all people in process, but one thing you may be thinking – the "I'm all alone in this" type of pain we all sometimes feel, that part is just plain false. You are not alone. We are not alone. I promise.

And here's another promise: there is hope and you truly can be whole again – or maybe even for the first time.

So, what do you say? Let's start at the beginning . . .

CHAPTER 2

EASTER IN OZ

God, I don't want to live in brokenness but in restoration.
I commit this journey to you. Please hug my mom and dad for me and
tell them that I love them and can still see their faces. Tell them I can see their
eyes. Tell them I can still see their faces, and that I see them in the kids.

On Good Friday 1999, my mom and dad came to Ferndale, Michigan, where my little girl Alex and I were living. We went to dinner at an all-you-can-eat Chinese buffet. My parents did a number of things I think grandparents pride themselves in. They picked up the check and they played *I've got your nose* with two-year-old Alex – normal stuff that we all take for granted. As my 30th birthday was less than a month away, they poked around to find out if there was anything special that I might really need. They decided to get me a new mattress.

"It's part of your healing," Mom said.

She was a social worker. In my teens, I would protest, "Quit shrinking me, Mom!" But she was right. I'd been sleeping on a fold up hideaway bed since Alex's dad left. Maybe it would be healing to have a bigger bed. Maybe it wouldn't feel so empty now, this year and some months after the devastating split.

"Get her a mattress and the box spring, and get a frame. Get everything," my father said "Go with your mom and pick it out. Get a good one. It'll last longer. Don't get junk."

He loved classic, quality things – real leather, hand blown glass, natural fabric. If there was one thing my daddy was NOT, it was fake. After dinner we went back to the hotel for some swimming. Now, Mom was a water safety instructor in high school and was bent on teaching Alex to swim that weekend.

"Oh, she'll be a fish by the time we go home. Just watch," she said, and they popped into the water. As Mom and Alex held onto the sides of the pool and practiced. "Kick, kick, kick, kick," Moms voice echoed off the atrium walls. "And blow bubbles! Bbbbbb! Like a little tug boat! Bbbbbb!"

I remembered the way she taught me the same thing. I even re-member my swimming suit – dark blue, with a yellow ducky. I know. You're jealous. We can't *all* have ducky suits.

When they were "turning into prunes" they hopped out of the pool and wrapped up in towels.

"Do you guys want to spend the night here?" Mom said? "There's a whole extra room!"

"No thanks, Mom," I said. "I think I just want to crash at home."

"How about Alex? Do you want HER to spend the night?"

"No. That's OK."

"Why, baby?"

"We'll just see you in the morning."

We made plans for the weekend, especially for them to come to my house for brunch after they went to Easter service. Mom kissed me on the cheek and hugged me goodbye like a neighbor, not a beloved daughter. She was hurt and Dad was hiding. He didn't show his face.

I used to see a therapist who had a sign on her wall that said, "Life's Messy."

I spent a lot of money on that lady, and the best thing I took away was from that sign. Life *is* messy. It always is. People are messy. Families are messy. Relationships are messy. We are all a beautiful, terrible mess. Me too. Mom too. Dad too.

I think there's a chance Daddy had an undiagnosed something. My brother and I think maybe Asperger's. Dad was brilliant. He was often kind, but he could also be very mean sometimes. He threw me into a wall once for vacuuming the wrong way. Once, child protective services came to ask me questions. I remember that day. I was in my front yard chopping a cord of wood. That chopping was my best summertime workout and helped my family, as the wood heated our home in the cold northern winters in Michigan's frigid Upper Peninsula. The fancy men in suits driving a stylish car asked, "Does your dad ever hit you? Your brother? Your mom? Do you feel safe in your home? Would you tell us if something was going on?" And I said, "No. No. No. Yes and yes." I had no idea what in the world they were doing at my house. I thought every house was messed up like mine. I really thought we were normal. Maybe we were, and if so, that is just plain sad.

I still don't really know if my family was normal. I do know that it was not my choice as a kid growing up, but that I wasn't a kid anymore that night. I *had* a kid and I didn't want her to stay with them at that hotel. I resented that, too. I resented not being able to trust them.

Dad's drinking was also a little out of control. Probably mom's, too. I can't remember a single day that they didn't knock back a couple martinis after work, and they drank wine with dinner every day. It was "good for your health," after all, but sometimes it made my father pass out and sometimes it made him even weirder.

Please understand, I loved my dad, but he was broken, and I was hurt and angry. And my Mom? I don't know if she knew what she could do beyond love us all and pray.

Mom called Easter morning to make sure I hadn't changed my mind about going to church with them. I told her I'd need the time at home to get the meal prepared, as they wanted to be back on the road by 2:00. She agreed that was a good plan but made me promise to wait on her for Alex's Easter egg hunt. I promised, adding that we'd watch the Easter Veggie Tale video since we couldn't make mass.

I'd had it with church in those days. I thought it was bunk. I'd had a few encounters with God, as I understood Him at that point in my life, but none of them in a church. In fact, I was quite confident that a church would be the least likely place I'd connect with my creator. At that point, I knew nothing whatsoever about the resurrection, had no understanding of what it meant or why it mattered. Plus, I wanted to assert my adult self. I wanted to make my own choice and have my parents accept it for a change.

If I had to do it over again I would have gone to church with them that day.

After the service, they came to my bungalow just off Woodward Avenue and we all ate a beautiful Easter dinner with everything our Syrian family enjoyed. We had kabobs stacked high with grilled mushrooms and onions, marinated beef, the most buttery rice pilaf, stuffed grape leaves, yogurt and cucumber salad.

Our pita was huge as my head and my younger brother Ryan jammed his full of tabouli and garlic sauce. There was red sauce with onion, garlic, clove; cinnamon, black pepper and red wine over French style green beans. It was a feast! I admit the baklava was store-bought, *cuz, ain't nobody got time for that*!

I most remember the kibbeh Mom made and brought with them.

My grandma, my father's mother, taught my mother two things before she "let that Polish-Irish girl marry her son." She taught her how to cook and how to swear in Arabic. As a result, the kibbeh was delicious. Lamb and bulgur wheat on the bottom, stuffed with sautéed pine nuts and onion. My mother passed that on to my daughter.

"Look, Baby," she said "You can pull the top off the kibbeh! See the nuts in there? Try a nut. Mmmmmm," and she put a plop of the yogurt sauce on the filling and put the top back on.

Try it," she said.

"Mmmmm! Gooooood," Alex said "Minty!"

"Yes, baby girl, minty! There's mint in the cucumber yogurt sauce!" Mom turned to me. "She has a discerning palate, Shan!" and my heart swelled with a mother's pride and a daughter's love.

As we ate our Easter meal that day, my father commented on how much our Arabic feast was like what Jesus would have eaten. He, being Syrian, always loved to point out how close to Jesus we are on the family tree.

"Jesus was our next door neighbor," he'd say. "He probably looked a lot more like me than that statue at church this morning. Blonde Jesus, my foot! He probably had a nose like ME!"

Dad was actually mixed, half something West European and half Syrian, but he looked 100% Arab: dark hair, olive skin, green eyes, huge nose.

"Lord, he probably had a nose like my MOTHER!" he added.

Grandma had an epic nose.

Ryan put down kabob after kabob as he shared about his upcoming lacrosse season.

"Coach is tough, man, but we're gonna cream the other guys this year. It's gonna be a good one."

My mom and dad said the team was perfect, which didn't surprise me. Ryan was (and still is) nearly perfect. By God's grace I've never been jealous of him. He's an amazing brother. He's a total jock in the very best possible sense of the word. And he's a boss. He is just like Daddy was, without the dysfunction, or disorder or disease.

I cleared the table of the dishes and went to the kitchen to clean them up as Mom asked Alex, "Do you want to play a game?"

"Yes! Yes!" she said bouncing up and down until her long brown hair flew through the air.

"Oh good, you little jumping bean! What should we play?"

"*Wizard of Oz! Wizard of Oz!*"

Alex and I had just seen the play the week before so we'd been playing *lots* of *Wizard of Oz*. Alex went to put on her ruby slippers and magic wands and laid plastic emeralds all over her bedroom floor to represent the Emerald City. "I'll be Dorothy!" she said. "You be the witch!"

"The wicked witch or the good witch?"

"Both, silly," she said. "And Grandpa *you* be Oz, OK, and Uncle Ryan is the Lion."

I watched from the kitchen as they gleefully went scene by scene.

"Spin, spin, spin!" Alex directed and they went round and round on the living room floor and landed on their bottoms into the Land of Oz.

"You've got quite a little director here, Shan," Mom said, full of pride.

Glasses and plates clinked as I dried and put them away. I heard Daddy singing in his deepest voice "Oh Ye Oh… Waaaay Oh," like the guards in the movie did.

"Good! Grandpa! Uncle Ryan, ROAR!"

"But I'm too scared to roar." Ryan shivered. Even he was getting into the spirit of it!

"Pretend!"

"Keep singing, Grandpa! Sing!"

Daddy had a beautiful voice. I have such fond memories of him singing in church on Christmas. "O Holy Night" was his favorite. Mine, too. I loved to hear him sing and to play the piano. He was brilliant. It was the best stuff of childhood. Dad may have fought with me or mom, but when I'd lay myself in bed at night, I'd often hear him on the piano downstairs. It soothed me. It soothed us all.

For all of our differences, music was one area where daddy and I did connect. Dad's record collection was massive and diverse, spanning everything from Air Supply and the Beatles, to Vivaldi to Led Zeppelin. He had Kenny Rogers and The Jackson 5 and tons of bluegrass. He taught me how to take care of records and I'm pretty positive my career in radio is closely connected to having him as my dad.

No matter how tight money got when I was a kid, daddy would always find room in the budget for music and we loved going to the record store together. Oh how I miss the record store! My kids are like, "What's a record store?" but to me it was a safe space. The record store was the perfect place for us because we didn't talk, but it wasn't too quiet. It was off-beat, like us. Dad and I loved this place, the music. It was the great equalizer. It was our happy place.

Of course, dad had a mean set of speakers. Back in the 80s, it was *the bigger, the better* when it came to stereo speakers, and his were as tall as me. When I got bigger and the speakers got smaller, dad kept up with the trends and wired our living room up like a recording studio. He loved to crank it up. I can't wait to meet him in heaven one day, all healed and whole and restored. I can't wait to finally see him free. My best music memories, though, were when he took me on daddy/daughter dates to see Broadway shows when the tours came to my childhood homes of Washington D.C. and Minneapolis.

We saw *Fiddler*. The best parts of daddy were a lot like Tevye.

We saw Marvin Hamlisch's, *They're Playing Our Song.*

The ultimate, though, was *Jesus Christ Superstar.* We saw it twice.

Now, I know that there are many Christians who were very offended by *Jesus Christ Superstar.* Some say it's unholy, but we were not among them. For my family, *Superstar* drew us each in our own ways into a deeper understanding of who Jesus was, who He loved, who he came to save, and why He was killed. Plus, it just plain rocked.

"Hey, Put," dad said as he reached for the olive tray at dinner one night. *Put* was his nickname for me from when I was learning to walk and instead just "putted around." "You haven't seen my George Carlin *Class Clown* record have you?"

"No Daddy," I said, shrugging and looking away.

"Or my Don McClean *American Pie?*"

"Nope, haven't seen them," I said as I passed Ryan the tossed salad.

I was lying. They were inside the cabinet behind him, between my B52s and Depeche Mode. I just didn't want to give them up.

"Isn't this nice," Mom said. "See? Even though we can't always see each other, we stay together! Kids, I want you to know how much I love you. How much I wish we could always be together. I wish, Daddy and I do, that we could give you so much more."

Ryan and I assured them they didn't need to give us more. They'd given us so much. Our education. Their love.

Why is she saying this stuff? I thought. Our parents don't say things like that. They were the type of parents who always pushed us to stand on our own two feet. Plus, it sounded strangely final. Daddy just sat there silently chewing the stem of his pipe and tapping the golden handle of his walking stick. *Why isn't he chiming in?* I thought, *What is going on?*

And then my mother pulled a ring off her hand and handed it to me. The giant black opal ring was a gift to her from my dad. He had it made for her. I don't remember the reason, if it was Christmas or for an anniversary. I do remember that dad purchased the stone from a gemologist in Washington D.C. when I was 10 years old and that he held off for another 10 years before having it set.

"No point in having this gem put in a bad setting," he said. "An artist needs to do this, a good artist. Sometimes you just have to wait for the right one."

The right one was an amazing jeweler from the Renaissance Festival circuit who crafted a bold setting of gold iris filigree. It was stunning.

Mom said: "Here, take it. I really want you to have it."

My head was shaking back and forth like one of those dog toy bobble heads people put in the rear window of cars.

"No! Mom, what are you talking about? I can't even picture your hand without it."

"*Please.* Take it," she said and she started to put it on my finger.

"Mom," I said, "I'll have it one day."

That was the only time mom and I ever confessed the truth that one day she would die and that one day I'd wear her ring. One day I would look down at my hand and her ring would smile back at me. Like all women do as they don their mom or grandma's rings. I would miss my mom like women always do. I would wonder when I'd turned *old* and when my hand started to look exactly like hers. With that, it was dessert and espresso, then mom and dad loaded up the big blue van and with hurried goodbyes, they hit the road to beat the Easter rush.

The fact that she instinctively wanted to give that ring to me then, at dinner, made me think that she knew something was up; that she sensed a "disturbance in the force." That was confirmed by what happened the night before they died.

I was in bed reading a wonderful book full of distant and exotic adventures. I was *hooked.*

The phone rang, jarring me out of the world I was in. It was Mom, and her voice was exhausted. She smokes too much, I thought. I wish she'd quit.

"Hi sweetie. What are you doing?" She asked.

"I'm reading a book," I said. "Can I call you when I get to the end of the chapter?"

"Sure. I love you."

"I love you, too."

Click.

Ring.

Mom again.

"Hey, Mom."

"Hi, sweetie."

"What's going on Mom?"

"Oh, nothing. I just want to talk to you."

"OK, Mom. Well, let me call you right back. I'm really into this book and it's almost the end of the chapter."

Now, understand that this is rare for me. I've been dyslexic and for much of my life I could not get *into* books. I remember thinking at the time, wow this is ironic. Mom's the one who asks to call *me* back at the end of the chapter, and now it's me. It's happening – the inevitable is happening. I am turning into my mother!

Ring.

"Hello?" It was Mom, again.

"Hi, Shan. I just wanted to talk with you."

"It's OK, Mom. What did you want to talk about?"

"No, you know what? It's OK. I'm just gonna go to bed. I love you, honey. I'll just talk to you tomorrow."

"Are you sure?"

"Yeah, I'm sure. I love you, baby."

"I love you, too, mom."

"Good night."

"Good night."

I finished my chapter and went to sleep, only to be awakened at 4:00 a.m. by the ring of the phone again.

Wow, she wants to talk early, I thought.

But it wasn't mom. It was my friend Rob. Rob and I met doing standup comedy at Go Banana's Comedy club in Cincinnati just after college. We did a talk show together for a short while back then. He said, "You might want to call your parents. There's been a tornado near their house."

Not awake enough to understand the urgency, I said, "No, they're OK. I just spoke with Mom last night. I'll call her a little later. It's too early."

"No!" Rob said, "You don't understand. This JUST HIT and it hit right by your parents' house! You should call now. Sycamore High School took it in the teeth."

Sycamore was less than a block from Mom and Dad. I thanked Rob and immediately called Mom but it really felt more like doing due diligence than an emergency.

The phone rang and rang and rang with no answer. That was strange. No answer *and* no answering machine. Even if they were still sleeping, why wouldn't the machine pick up? No voice mail? What was UP with that?

So, I called Ryan.

"Hey Bud, sorry to wake you, but there's been a tornado by mom and dad's and I can't get them on the phone."

"Oh my God!" Ryan said. His reaction was the first time I realized that something significant could be unfolding.

We decided the best course of action was for me to go into the radio station where I worked as a traffic reporter and for him to make tracks for Cinci and call me when he got to the house. My wonderful friend and nanny, LaJeana came over to be with Alex and I beat it to the office. My coworkers became "Johnny on the spot" reporters as we called police emergency numbers, local fire departments, EMS and TV Station news rooms and the Red Cross disaster relief line, trying to figure out where the Cook family was.

I could hear the calls weaving between the traffic reports my co-horts were trying to give.

Over and over I told whoever was on the line: "7575 Cornell Rd. Lee and Jacque Cook."

We heard they were fine and had relocated to a nearby gym.

We heard the house was gone.

We heard it was damaged.

I heard everything except the voice of my parents.

We were running out of options, running out of ideas, when Ryan called. I will never forget that conversation:

"Hi… um, Shannyn… this is Ryan."

I know who this is, I thought, *why was he acting so weird?* So "official?"

"Um, yeah, you remember Mom and Dad?"

"What do you MEAN? Of course I remember mom and dad! What are you talking about?"

"Well, they're dead."

I felt like I'd been sucked into a black hole. My jaw clenched so hard I almost broke my teeth. My heart stopped. As I sat still in my office chair, I felt like I was spinning round and round and round. My brain was on fire. My eyes felt like jelly.

"What? What do you mean? Are you sure? Have you seen them?"

"No," he said. "I haven't seen them. But they're dead."

Ryan sounded like a two year old doing his best grown man voice. "I'm standing here in the back of an ambulance with the guy who took care of them."

"Took *care* of *them*? What are you talking about? Is he there? Right, there? Let me talk to him! Can I talk to him?"

"Sure," Ryan said in the same serious voice and handed the phone over to a paramedic.

He had a military monotone voice that was somehow a comfort compared to Ryan's disconnected voice. "Miss Cook. I'm sorry to say it was your parents."

"How do you know?" I said. "Did a family member identify them?"

"No ma'am, they were positively identified by your neighbor. I'm sorry for your loss."

I think I thanked him.

27

I told my brother I'd be down as fast as I could and set down the phone. Its click was like the closing of an airless vault.

But I wasn't in a vault. And I wasn't alone. I was still in a busy room full of open microphones that were getting ready to do live traffic feeds to radio stations across Detroit. That meant I... couldn't... scream.

I rose from my chair.

I could feel my pulse in my tongue. My lips were numb and my breath short. I got up from my cubicle and tried to make my way to the bathroom to puke. I almost made it, but I felt a stab in my gut that brought me to my knees. Thoughts collided in my head like bumper cars.

Unreal! You really *do* fall down on the floor when you find out terrible news. *My parents are dead.*

I cannot believe I'm actually on my knees, on the floor in my office. *Oh, my God! My parents are dead.*

Who is with me? Is this my boss's hand on my shoulder?" *Somebody help me – my parents are dead.*

This is so strange: I really can't walk. *My. Parents. Are. Dead.*

I just lay there in a heap on the floor and wept silently until my coworkers walked me to the couch in the break room. This is crazy, I thought. People actually *do* bring you to a couch to lay down when you lose it.

All I could say was, "I need to go down there. I need to get down there."

My boss, Phil Lemka, said he'd get me a plane ticket and I could be in Cincinnati in 3 hours.

But I didn't think I could fly right then. I didn't want to deal with an airport. I didn't think I could keep my cool. My thoughts collided again.

I have to drive. Can I drive? Can I drive myself? Is this real? Can it be true? There must be a mistake. How could they be sure it's my parents who were killed? Their friends aren't there. No family to say it was in fact them. They didn't know their neighbors *that* well.

Yet my brother said they were dead and he would absolutely not kid about this. He wouldn't.

He didn't.

It was true.

I couldn't run from it. I couldn't get around it.

The only choice Ryan and I had was to walk right straight through it.

Even then, I thought how hard it must have been for Ryan to deliver that news. The same news I now had to tell Alex. How would *she* handle it? I could barely process how I was feeling about all this and she was only three. And my grandmas! Oh how could I tell my poor grandmothers their first-borns were gone?

As I slouched on the couch, I could just barely hear the conversation my coworkers were having with my boss over the conversation I was muttering to myself, "Who am I going to call? Who in the world gives a rip about me anymore? Who cares if I need help? I need help. *Help!*"

It's weird, isn't it? The way life goes on even in those times when it will never be the same. Weird, how people still carry on like normal and complain about their husbands and parents, even when your husband is leaving or your parent dies. They still grab a coffee, get a haircut, watch a movie, order a pizza, punch a clock and pick the kids up like the world is still turning, even when in your heart you know the world isn't turning. Not anymore, never again, not in your world. Your world is over.

Meanwhile, reports went out from our studios, "In 3, 2, . . . I-75 southbound slow as you head to the 375 interchange. Expect delays as well on the inbound M-10."

I worked with a girl named Lorna Stephens. She was one of those people who was super, super into angels. She had an angel pin and purse and necklace, an angel hanging from her review mirror of her car, which had an angel bumper sticker that said "Angels on Board." She helped me hold my head up when Alex's dad left me. She'd been a single mom, too. She survived, thrived, remarried. She'd given me hope and she was one of the coworkers hovering over me as I mumbled like a bag lady to myself. This is it, I thought. This is how people unhinge. I was like a fatal freeway crash causing a nasty gawker delay in my own office.

"I've got to get out of here," I said.

"I'll drive you, honey," Lorna said. And we left.

It was nasty, grey and rainy, and I knew I was on the edge of the very same storm that had just erased any proof of my family, *except for Ryan and me,* off the map. When we got to the purple door of my bungalow I choked on my own breath. LaJeana Kennedy swung the door open wide. Lorna zipped up to the porch and whispered the news to my sweet babysitter, who quickly gathered her bag to leave. Meeting me on the sidewalk, she gave me the sternest, most knowing look. "Oh, honey," she said. "I am so sorry." Her whisper warmed my check and the cool air whipped by.

"Let me know how I can help. It's gonna be OK." Her eyes locked to mine. "I promise." And with that, she hopped into her mommy van and drove off.

I have to tell someone now, I thought. I have to tell my daughter that her grandparents are gone. God help me. What do I say?

I just spit it out. "Alex, mommy has sad news, but it's happy news, too," I said, crouching down and taking her little hands in mine. "Grandma Jacque and Grandpa Lee are in heaven, baby. I'm sorry to say, sweetheart, that they were killed in a big, big tornado."

"Like in *Wizard of Oz*, Mommy?"

"Yes baby, like in *Wizard of Oz*. They are over the rainbow," I was steady and calm.

"It's OK, Mommy." And she seemed to not just understand, but instantly accept. I wanted to be like her. I could not. The best I could do was pretend to be OK, which I definitely was not.

"You know what, sweetheart, it doesn't seem like it now, but one day it will be OK again."

This was a full-blown lie. I was making up a fairy tale for my baby girl. I most certainly did not believe it would ever be anything like *OK* because I was her mom and I was now a total mess. I felt worse for her than I felt for Ryan or myself. She had John for a dad – brilliant, yes, but tortured and seemingly in love with his own pain. And she had a broken-down me for a mom. My only hope was that *the universe* (that's how people who don't know Christ often refer to God) would do a miracle. Thankfully, I still believed in miracles.

I told her I had to go to Cincinnati for a couple of days and that I would be home soon. I explained that she'd go to daddy and grandma's house until I came home. I promised I'd be back soon, but that there was a big mess where grandma and grandpa's house used to be and mommy had to go help clean it up.

I had no idea how true that was going to be. So we packed her little Barbie suitcase with her jammies and her favorite blanket as her daddy pulled up. "I'm so sorry," he said, as I cracked my front door to let him in. "I can drive you down."

"Are you kidding me?" I said, turning venomous, still angry from his abandonment. "The last thing in the world I need night now is a four hour drive with a man who does not believe in God."

"OK," he said, "I'm sorry, Shannyn."

He scooped up our baby girl in his arms. She blew me a little kiss. I gave her a giant hug and tons of kisses on her cheeks, nose and little bow of a mouth.

"I love you, baby. I love you so, so much. Mommy loves you so much. You know that, right? I love you and I will be back as soon as I can."

"OK, Mommy," she said, blowing a kiss my way over the back of her daddy's shoulder. They were off.

With a slam of the door, my house fell absolutely silent. I eased onto my couch. Fortunately, Lorna was still there.

"Mom and dad gave me this couch when John left," I said to Lorna. "I told them my couch felt too big with John gone and they had this one delivered to me, a love seat. They were not rich. They couldn't afford it but they did it anyway."

It was the first time I'd realized how sacrificial they were. How *much* they truly did support me. I'd never known they were there for me until they were gone.

"We should really get going, honey," Lorna said. "It's a long drive down. Are you all packed?"

I nodded. Lorna reached out to help me up. Clicking off the lights, she asked one more question, "Have you called your grand-mothers yet?"

"No." I said. "I don't know what to say. What do I say?"

"You just have to say it. You just have to tell them."

"Tell them their babies are dead?"

"Yes."

Now, I could understand the pressure my sweet Ryan was under as he called me. I rallied all the strength within me and dialed my grandma, Mary.

"Hello?" she said with her typical feisty voice.

"Hi, Grandma. It's Shannyn."

"Shannyn! Hello! How are you?"

"I'm good Grandma, but I have bad news. Are you sitting down?" I could not believe that I asked her that, but it seemed appropriate, as she was aging and a little frail. A fall could truly hurt her. "Are you?"

"No."

"Well, please sit down for me, OK? I love you. Are you sitting down?"

I could see her kitchen in my mind. The telephone on the wall. An egg timer to make sure she never talked more than five minutes. A ruler to smack you if you were sassy. Tongs to grab Syrian bread from the toaster next to her stool.

"Yes. I'm sitting."

"Grandma. There's been a tornado in Cincinnati."

"*Ya Hayenti!*" (Which means "Oh, My God" in Arabic)

"And Grandma, there's more. Grandma…" I looked to Lorna for strength, and she nodded, "Grandma, Daddy's dead."

"WHAT?" She screamed at the top of her lungs "WHAT? JIM! JIM! Get in here!"

I could hear Grandpa shouting: "What is it?"

"It's Shannyn. She says Leon is dead!"

And then, the phone dropped to the floor.

Grandpa picked it up and I then told him that his first-born son was gone.

"Oh my," he said. "Oh my. Yes, yes, OK. Well, thank you for calling honey."

"Grandpa, I'm leaving for Cincinnati right now. I'll call you when I get there to let you know more. I'm so sorry, Grandpa. I'm so, so sorry. I wish it wasn't true, but it is. I'll call Uncle Ray to let him know. I love you guys. I love you so much and it's going to be OK. I promise."

"OK, baby. Call us when you get there."

He was clearly in shock.

Hanging up the phone, I slid to my kitchen floor weeping, "How do people DO this? I can't call my other Grandma. I can't!"

"Does your mom have any siblings?" Lorna asked.

"Yes."

I called my Uncle Tim. He was my favorite uncle. When I was five years old, I cried myself to sleep because mom explained to me that I could never grow up and marry Uncle Tim. Now it was my turn to break his heart and tell him that his older sister had just been murdered by a freak windstorm.

"OK, baby. It's gonna be all right," he said to me. I chose to believe him. "I'll call Uncle Mark, Aunty Mickey and Greg. One of us will tell Grandma. We'll leave right away. We'll meet you there."

Still sitting cross-legged on my kitchen floor, I tried to stand and hang up the phone, but couldn't find the strength to make my body move. I knew why people unraveled and sat in corners and rocked back and forth or banged their heads on walls. It was what I wanted to do, and yet I did not want to be that girl. I needed to be more. I had to meet Tim and my brother. I rallied myself to my feet and hung up the phone and just as it hit the carriage, it rang again.

It was LeJeana. She had tragically lost her beautiful daughter Sammie in a pedestrian car accident about two years prior. She was walking across the street holding her little hand as a car came out of nowhere and ran right into Sammie, ripping her from LaJeana's grasp and killing her instantly within one week after her ninth birthday. The night before her birthday party, Sammie told me the only thing she wanted for her ninth birthday...was to turn 10.

"Hi Jeanie," I said.

"Honey, I don't know what's going on, but I swear I just heard Sammie's voice and she said, 'Tell Shannyn that her mom and dad are OK. So... I'm... telling you?'" She was tentative as if to say, "I know this is crazy, but..."

I just gasped. I couldn't speak. I know now about the great cloud of witnesses that surround us, but at the time, I was in uncharted territory. "I'm so sorry," she said. "But I know they're OK."

"I'm so sorry for *YOU*," I cried back, "I'm so, so sorry, Jeanie. I'm so sorry about Sammy."

"I'll be OK, Shannyn. You can make it. You're not alone. We are here for you, honey. Call me when you get back or if you need anything, OK?"

I promised I would and thanked her again. Hanging up the phone, it instantly started to ring again and I chose not to answer.

Lorna had bleach blonde hair that looked like a fairy princess and a gentle voice to go with it. Today, she was my Glinda. Today, she'd help me to follow the yellow brick road all the way home. Whatever home was – or whatever it was not anymore.

"You need to pack something to wear at the funeral, honey," she said. "Something you never want to wear again."

This was wisdom.

I grabbed a long black velvet dress and a black jacket, while my thoughts continued on their collision course.

My mom got this for me. She gave it to me. She said it would look beautiful. She said…

"What do you want to put in their caskets?" Lorna said.

"What do you mean?" I said.

I'd never heard of such a thing, but the memory of their Easter visit was vivid, so I grabbed Alex's big plastic emeralds, the ones which had just covered her bedroom floor when they'd played pretend Emerald City. I shoved a few into the pocket of my backpack.

"We should get going, honey. It's getting a little late."

She was right. I was going to have to do this. I was going to have to *go there.*

I remember stopping for gas station snacks – warm cashews. I thought, "I'll probably hate these forever now."

I remember thinking, "I'm going to look so old after this."

I remember the strange sensation of driving though the rain and knowing it was the edge of the same storm that killed my mom and dad.

I remember the music on the radio and how I *knew* each song was a message from the other side just to me. I remember the Otis Redding song "Sitting on the Dock of the Bay." I knew they were fine, somehow. I knew it and at the same time I began to question my sanity.

"Pray with me, Lorna," I said.

"You pray, honey."

I started.

"Our Father, who art in heaven, hallowed be thy name." It was the only thing I could think of, but we went on and on and on with that mantra until we finally neared mom and dad's neighborhood and were welcomed by a police blockade. I told Lorna what house we needed to go to. She rolled down the window.

"Yes, officer," she said in her floating Glinda voice, "we need to get to that house up there, about a block in."

"I'm sorry, ma'am but not tonight, you're not," he said, "Please turn your car around."

I got all bold and said something like, "Oh, yes we are! We're going right around this corner and parking in front of that house."

I pointed at the home of the Johnsons. That was where Ryan said we'd meet up with my uncles to spend the night.

"Can I see your I.D., ma'am?"

"What?"

Lorna gently grabbed my arm and laid her gentle voice on the officer again. "Sir, we are in town from Detroit. This is Shannyn Cook. Her parents were killed in the tornado. We just need to get her to her family's meeting point, right there at the Johnson's.

"All right. But don't you go anywhere. This city's in lock down."

The Johnsons were the leaders of Ryan's high school Young Life group – an evangelical youth outreach and discipleship organization. They led my brother to the Lord when he was 14. My family thought they were in a cult, but a harmless one. They weren't a cult, of course, but I was about to have my first interaction with real live Evangelicals.

"Oh grrrreeeaaaat," I thought as that occurred to me. As if things weren't bad enough, now *THIS!* I was sure they'd be all syrup-sweet and pat my shoulder and say stuff like, "God has a plan," and "God is good," and I'd have to resist the impulse to drink or smack someone.

They were all in the basement – the Young Life kids, the youth group – sitting in a circle and praying. But it wasn't like any prayer I'd ever heard. Certainly not like the five hundred repetitions of the *Our Father* Lorna and I had recited all the way from Detroit. They seemed to be sort of free forming it. One person would just say something like, "Comfort Ryan, Lord." and then everyone else would chime in, "Yes, Lord" and "Please, Father." I didn't know what to do with that, at all.

I went upstairs to meet my uncles, Tim and Mark, and my cousin Greg. They were like a super hero team. Like a triage unit. Like special forces. They were on it.

Making phone calls to banks and insurance agents and hotels.

Calling the funeral homes and cemeteries.

They were hooking it up! They'd just lost their sister and cousin, and still, they were full steam ahead. They were much better at the *adult thing* than I was at the time.

I didn't put this together then, of course, but it's cool, isn't it? How God gives us our natural gifts and how they work together to help us all. Uncle Mark is naturally gifted at stuff like insurance and business-y paperwork. Greg, a lawyer, reads all those lines of legalese and thinks, *oh yes* or mercy no! It makes sense to him. He thinks ahead in the same way a choral singer reads ahead in the music so he's prepared for the high notes. We were all definitely stretching our range that night.

And so, they made calls. Ryan prayed with his youth group. I called my ex to tell him I was safe and then went to bed to listen for the Lord in hopes He'd make sense of it all for me. No dreams came that night.

In the morning, I woke to find Ryan on the couch next to me. It was still very early, maybe 5:30. He was reading from his black and worn-out soft cover Bible.

He quietly read and then he closed the crinkly pages and said, "You know what? I do this thing called a Daily Devotional. My girlfriend and I do it together. We read the same scriptures on the same day. It's mapped out for us." Wiping the sleep from my eyes, I tried to politely absorb my dear brother's Christianese.

"You know what today's Scripture was? It's the story about the empty tomb. When Jesus's people go to where they think the body is and it's gone. Kinda neat, huh? Considering?"

"Yeah, neat," was all I could think of to say. I was grateful his Bible was giving him the peace I lacked and longed for. But I was certain that I wasn't going to find it in those pages. Not me, a divorced, arty-party chick.

The house was too quiet, so we turned on the TV. It was the news. There stood a reporter in her blue blazer and perfect helmet-hair all propped up for her live shot... from our driveway.

"Hey, look, that's their van!" I said, "That is our van, right?"

The snazzy blue minivan, the nicest vehicle we'd ever owned, the one that had just ushered them home from our Easter feast, was flipped over and tossed aside. Mom's car was parked in the driveway untouched, just waiting for someone to emerge from the now-gone garage and zip off to work in it.

"Weird. Look at Mom's car," I said. "It's perfect. But where's the house?"

"It's gone, Shannyn."

"All gone?"

"Pretty much, yep."

"I'm scared, Ryan," I said.

"Me, too," he said and went back to reading his devotional as I pulled out a notebook and pen and wrote:

I hate this day because I wish I would have put down the book and talked with my mom.

I'm so mad right now and I feel so ripped off.

I hate this, I can't do this! I want my mom! I want to shout and cry, "My God, my God! Why have your forsaken me?" I barely even know who you are. I barely even know who I am. All I really know is this: I am my mother's daughter and I am lost.

The first thing we had to do that morning was attend a meeting held at a local church by the American Red Cross. It was organizational and a total blur, like Charlie Brown's teacher: "Wa wa, wawa-wawa."

And I started to think, so, *this* is what shock feels like. Strange. I'm still in it. I didn't think shock would last this long.

We were issued laminated passes, which gave us access to our block and house. I remember thinking, *a pass* to get to *my* house?

But we were not in charge – at all. So I hung my pass around my neck, like a VIP credential, but all the VIPs… well, they were… dead.

The media was there, too, and I began to see my own industry in an entirely new light. This was not about connecting the public with information. There was glitz and excitement. A reporter getting "hot and ready to go," like actors just before they burst on stage for their audition monologue. The story was national news – so my family's death could be somebody's big break.

It was ugly. It left me wondering about my profession, because these people were my next career step, one step past traffic reporter. They were TV reporters and they reeked of gum, greed and hairspray. It was like the intersection of a crime scene and the Miss America pageant.

As I looked on I realized a few things:

I probably wouldn't be able to do my same job when I got home, and certainly not in the same way.

I was cold, very cold and in my haste I hadn't packed a jacket.

We went outside to wait for a Red Cross bus to shuttle us to what we would then begin to refer to as *the address*. I avoided anyone with a camera and went outside the church doors and into the wind. A frail middle-aged woman with a Red Cross name badge stood nearby finishing a phone call.

"I'm sorry about your parents," she said as she hung up. "I work for the Red Cross. If there's anything you need, just say so."

I nodded.

"I lost my parents, too," she said. "When I was a teenager."

"I'm so sorry," I said. Realizing that I could barely put a sentence together I spit out one last thing, "I'm cold."

"There is a coat inside. I'll get you one," she said, and as if by magic she did. It was a beige trench that fit just right. It smelled like old lady and it gave me not just warmth, but hope. I needed a coat and the Red Cross produced one – from inside a church even. I got one for free. That was what beautiful looked like to me, like an old lady's trench coat on the back of the broken. In this case... me.

Now bundled up, I boarded the shuttle to home.

CHAPTER 3

SACRED GROUND ZERO

God, I wish I could have been there with Mom when she died.
If I'd been there, I'd lie next to her and I'd stroke her hair. I'd stroke
her face. I'd tell her how much I love her. I'd tell her she did a great job.
I'd hold her and pray for her out loud until she breathed her last and
I'd scream in the sunrise, "NO!"

The air smelled like dirt and rain and chainsaw oil as the doors of the van swung open.

None of us spoke. It was one of those rare heart-in-your mouth moments – the rare times when you want to run and scream and shout "No, no, no!" Yet somehow you dig in. You move. There's a Hebrew proverb that says, "The heart moves the feet." That must be true because my head was saying, "No" even as I plodded forward.

I remembered my mom quoting Kipling's poem, –*If.* -"So hold on when there's nothing left within you but the will which says to them 'hold on'." That was all I could do.

We all shuffled down the rubbery shuttle bus stairs to the devastation—not our house—our address – 7575 Cornell Rd was completely erased. It was true. It wasn't hype and TV confusion or sensationalism. It was gone. They were gone.

It was over.

I wish right now that I could stop and say it was an "all things through Christ who strengthens me moment." Maybe. Maybe it was. I didn't know Him yet. But that doesn't mean it wasn't Him who gave me strength. It could have been. It sure was not strength of my own.

Even at that I could only stand there and say, "Oh, my God! It's all gone. It's totally, totally gone."

Our house, the one I'd brought Alex home from the hospital to, had vanished. There was nothing. The two story suburban brick ranch had been taken down to the very ground. It was gone.

The only way you knew what room you were in was the flooring. Hardwood—dining room. Tile—kitchen. Only a simple row of bricks lined the edges of our home's perimeter where the fireplace used to stand. I remembered cuddling newborn Alex by that fireplace when we first brought her home from the hospital. I could see Dad in his rocker smoking his pipe. Mom in the kitchen, smoking her Parliaments and cooking and singing and swinging her hips. Gone. Gone. Gone.

I waited for a second, assuming one of the more religious among us would suggest it, but when none did, I said it myself, "Let's pray, you guys."

Trying to find level ground that we could all gather on and finding none, the uncles and my brother kicked aside bricks and plaster from blown up walls and random kitchen cabinets that were not even from our home until a space was cleared. We joined our hands in a circle and bowed our heads. Tim led. "Lord, thank you for my sister. Thank you for Jacque and Lee. Guide us. Help us to find what we need to find. Amen"

"Amen," we all said. I wanted to stay and pray all day, but there was work to be done and nothing else, really, to be said. So, amen was the end and we let go of one another's hands.

"What do we do now?" I whispered to my brother.

"I don't know," he said with a shrug. "Try to find stuff, I guess."

So, I just started to wander and scan the ground. It reminded me of when I was little and I would study the blacktop for pretty rocks embedded inside. I'd find agates and crystals. Sometimes, on a really hot day, I could dig them out with a butter knife.

It was the way a kid will always spot the robin's egg or the special feather. It was that kind of a search. Trying to carve and keep proof of something beautiful stuck in the muck and mire. Except I wasn't looking for extra treasure, I was looking for any treasure.

Here's a hint for you and my prayer for you when you lose your parents: Don't fight about stuff. Stuff is nothing. In my case, a tornado decided for us what we'd keep.

Making my way across the wreckage of 2x4s, drywall and trees, my knees buckled and my thoughts began to race again.

Don't fall down.

Do not fall down.

Don't you dare fall.

Don't fall apart.

Your family does not need you to fall apart. You have to walk, Shannyn.

There were TV cameras everywhere and a TV chopper flying overhead. A newspaper photographer was on the roof of a neighbor's house.

I've never seen a lens that long, I thought. I bet he can take a close up of me from there.

I felt so violated. I didn't want to be seen. I did not want to worry about what I was going to LOOK like in the paper or on the evening national news. I wanted to hide, but there was nowhere *to* hide.

I couldn't run behind the house.

And then out of the corner of my eye, I caught a golden glint. Leaning down to look, I saw that it was the brass top of my dad's walking stick, the ball with a compass in it. I eased myself to the earth and grabbed it and dusted it off—spit-shining the dirt away, making it perfect in case it was the only thing I found to remember Daddy by.

But nearby, about an arm's length away, I saw the cane's bottom, cherry wood with inlay. Dad loved that walking stick.

"I will help you walk."

It was my father's voice. I heard it. "I will show you where to go."

Wow, this is weird, I thought. Was that just Daddy?

I knew it was. I didn't know what to make of it, but it happened, just the same.

Since then, I've had Christians insist to me that it could not have been my daddy's voice, that it could have been my imagination or even a demon. I can't argue with them. I can only tell you that my Bible says that these things are a mystery. I heard my dad and it gave me comfort. Maybe the Lord gave me that in some supernatural way, even though I had no concept of who He was. I don't understand it, but I can tell you it happened.

In fact there were more "God sightings." Many, many more.

The next thing I heard is best described as a "still small voice." I wish I could come up with a more original way to put it for you, but that's what it was—a still small voice saying, "Though I walk through the valley of darkness and the shadow of death, I will fear no evil, for you are with me. Your rod and your staff, they comfort me."

Let's be clear: I didn't know that Scripture at all yet, let alone that it was from Psalm 23, but my next thought was: *That's from the Bible. I couldn't have thought that thought up. I am hearing voices.* I knew that the Lord was near.

So it must have been the Lord who guided me across the street to the place where I found the center of the *Jesus Christ Superstar* album. All the vinyl was gone, the cover missing. But there in the sticks and leaves and debris was the very center of the album. I bent down to pick it up and as I looked at the telling picture of two angels, back to back arching toward heaven, I began to sing the song Dad and I had sung so many times:

Try not to get worried.

Try not to turn onto problems that upset you.

Oh, don't you know everything's all right.

Yes, everything's fine.

And we want you to sleep well tonight

Let the world turn without you tonight.

If you try, you'll get by, so forget all about us tonight. (1)

I fell to the ground and wept because I didn't want to let the world turn without them and yet, I couldn't stop it.

Now the jig's up, I thought. Somewhere those photographers are out there and they finally have their picture of the daughter on the ground weeping. It's a wrap. The media had spread like cockroaches when the lights came on. They were not there, or if they were, they were hidden in the corners.

Once I calmed myself down again, I found I was wondering why the Christian youth group who showed up to clear away the wreckage looked like they had stars in their eyes. It was the first time I'd seen where that saying came from. Looking into the eyes of the youth group and their leader was like looking out of the glass on the bridge of the Starship Enterprise. They were some starry-eyed people, I tell you, with humble servants' hearts in the most selfless of all possible ways and I wondered what that was about. I was thankful for their help, for the help of the Red Cross and for the help of the dozens of prisoners who had been released to help clear the debris, many of whom were in my basement retrieving what remained.

I remember being afraid that the rain would come and ruin the pictures I was trying to find.

I remember finding the coat my mother always wore in the mess of it all and picking it up and smelling it. It smelled like she was wearing it. It smelled like she was in it. I will never ever forget that smell—like cigarettes and Estee Lauder and dirt and good food and I wish I had kept it because it is the closest I will be to her until heaven. I wanted to wrap it around me or lie down on the earth and just cuddle it. I wanted to put it on or wear it all day, but it was a fox fur coat and I never was a girl for fur.

And it was totally, epically trashed.

There was no way to make it pretty again. I wish, though, I had kept it, just to have her smell and something to hug all the many, many times I've needed to hug her. I would have hugged IT but I let it go and kept on searching.

As my eyes scanned the floors back and forth, back and forth like one scans a beach for shells, I realized there were a lot of people here, and once more my thoughts ran wild.

I have to clean this floor. We have company.

I headed toward the basement where the cleaning supplies were stored, and that's when I heard the prisoners singing. I wondered if I'd be safe to go get the mop alone. I decided I would be and made my move. Then it came to me: that is not a sane thought. You do not need to mop the floor. That is not logical. Now you can crack up if you want to and no one would blame you. Anyone would go nuts under these circumstances.

I followed that thought to its end. They'll lock me in a hospital. I can just have a quiet life. I never have to speak again if I don't want. Insurance will pay for it, or disability. You can just go ahead and Ophelia out, Shannyn.

But then I remembered my daughter back at home. Alex needed me. She needed her mommy to smile again, like Glinda does, not melt like the Wicked Witch crying "Oh what a world...what a world!" She needed me to pull it together. My baby girl kept me sane that day.

It was midday now and we were all getting tired and hungry when a truck from the Red Cross showed up with boxed lunches. The sandwiches were so beautiful. Chicken salad with green grapes mixed in on good wheat bread. Strawberries dipped in chocolate. I couldn't eat, but I stopped the search to listen to people talk and rest for a minute. Pulling out a Marlboro light and lighting it up, I looked into the eyes of the youth group leader and wondered why he was there, what his agenda was, why he was so happy? Why did he smile ear to ear?

His eyes sparkled at me. "You shouldn't smoke, ya know. It'll kill ya."

Nodding, I walked away.

Our block had been declared a Federal Disaster Area and with that came things like tanks. Actual Army-looking tanks were rolling down my street. Prisoners in their orange jumpers were out of their cells and were helping with heavy lifting. One such prisoner was working in a group at the next door neighbor's house. Their home, only 20 feet away from Mom and Dad's, looked like a doll house. The front was completely torn away, exposing a perfect interior. The tea pot still sat on the lace covered table, just waiting for someone to come and fill a cup.

The stocky, power-lifter-looking felon shouted to me, "Hey! Was that your house?"

"Yeah!" I said.

"This your necklace?" he shouted, holding out a golden beauty. "You missing it? Come look!"

"Naw, it's not mine," I said, "But thanks, man."

"I got a roll of bills over here, too. You guys keep cash in your house?"

"Naw, no cash in our house."

People amazed me with their capacity for goodness.

From my basement, I heard a hymn rise up. A spiritual filled the air.

"Wade in the water," the prisoners sang. "Wade in the water, children. Wade in the water."

I had sung that song in 4th grade and I joined my voice to theirs, "God's gonna trouble the water."

The voices of those prisoners were deep and steady as they collected every item and passed it up the still intact basement stairs to the floor of the kitchen where more men were gently wrapping each item and packing it perfectly in boxes.

"It's your Christmas stuff," one orange-suited man said, "I'm glad you got to keep your Christmas stuff at least."

"Thank you," I said. "Yeah, that's good."

The worst times bring out the best in people. These men were perfect evidence of that. Anytime someone tries to tell me than man is intrinsically evil, I remember those men and think, "Man is intrinsically good. But the world—the world is broken into little tiny bits."

In the wreckage, I found an almost-complete set of my great grandma's fancy china.

It was like an Easter egg hunt, only I was finding egg shell china with roses and a golden stripe. How could this have made it? It was exactly what Mom would have given me if she could only choose one thing—that and her ring.

I also found her apron, the one she always wore. She got the quilted denim thing at the St. Barbara ladies' bazaar in the 80s and wore it every time she cooked or cleaned. It was caked, as everything was, in a spray of mud and dust. I've cleaned it well and wear it all the time, too. To be honest, it's pretty awful. There any many cuter aprons, but I don't care.

Mom's fancy lace tablecloth was there, too, and her wooden spoon and the cookbook my Syrian grandma had given her when she married dad. It had her hand written notes.

This time it was Mom's voice I heard. "This is how you will keep us alive. You will make the food and set the table and when you do, you will tell the story of who we were."

I thought once more that I might be losing my mind. But I said, out loud, "Yes, Mom."

If I wasn't losing my mind, something was surely happening to my mind. It felt like a tiny mason was in my brain laying a thick brick wall between these moments and my memory of them. It was as if my own brain was in a very systematic way editing for me, trying to protect me and I had no control at all over what *it* was choosing for me to remember. It was scary. I appreciated and resented it at the same time.

The daylight was starting to show signs of retreat and I hooked back up with my uncles and Ryan.

"How's everybody doing?" Timmy said.

We all said we were fine and then scanned each other's faces to see if there was anyone lying. We all passed the test. We really were all surprisingly OK. So we compared notes about what we found and did. Uncle Mark had been talking most of the day with the insurance guy and Greg had been to the bank and post office.

"Well, kids," Greg said, "look what came in the mail today. It's your daddy's patent."

Dad had spent the last four to five years in his office and at laboratories field-testing an Eco-friendly coating to resist an invasive and aggressive marine parasite called zebra mussels. He started the research because the little critters had been mucking up the water intake screens which he designed for a living. He thought that rather than finding a way to get them off, there must be a way to keep them from attaching to the screen in the first place. It seems he was correct. We opened the letter and read the patent for his coating- issued to him on Good Friday, while he was in Detroit for our last visit. He named the coating Jacquelyn, after Mom.

We all stood in silent amazement at the irony and hope mixed together before us.

Ryan then said he'd found a ton of baseball cards and some Star Wars stuff. He also found Dad's Air Force hat and duffle bag.

Tim produced a big green book from under his coat. It was the family phone book, which people actually needed before cell phones. "I had to cut it out with a chain saw," he said. "It was stuck under the staircase. I knew you guys would want this so you could let the rest of your Dad's family know. Plus, it's got all your dad's business contacts in there."

"You just wanted to use a chainsaw." Uncle Mark bumped his quarterback of a little brother with his slender shoulder.

We still needed to find Dad's computer. It had been upstairs in his office, but so far the only things that had been found from upstairs were . . . Mom, Dad and the family Bible, which was found in a farmer's field 45 miles north. If we had his computer, though, we could know what was going on with his business. With the patent arriving that day, we thought there may be something important to know in there. It was now or never.

Looking across the street and into the field of broken trees, I thought it looked like the Heidelberg project with its seemingly random order. Yet everything was being intentionally placed, shoes that had been hammered into the siding of houses and dirty baby doll heads and bike tires and pool cues and stuffed animals everywhere. Observing this mess, this beautiful wreck, I thought, God is the artist of this. What is He trying to say? I look across the street into the field of trees. Broken can't touch it. They were shattered like toothpicks, like twigs. That's where they found Daddy. He was impaled in the trees. And Mom was found across the street. No one could look at those trees and not see the cross of Christ.

And then I noticed them, the shrouds draped from the branches. Purple silk.

"Do you see that, Ryan?" I asked my brother.

"Yeah, shrouds, that's crazy." he said.

"I'm going to the purple stuff," I said. "I'm going there."

I climbed my way across the downed limbs all stacked one upon another, straight to the first purple shroud, which turned out to be someone's prom dress. Looking all around I saw... nothing. Nothing special. Nothing ours. For a moment I was just confused. I had fully expected to find dad's computer in perfect shape lying right there at my feet. But no. "Purple, purple, purple. Go to the purple," I muttered as I crunched across the tree parts to a lavender bathrobe, strewn in the mud and leaves. "Where is it, where is it?" By now darkness was really starting to fall. We wouldn't be allowed to stay after sundown and bulldozers were coming at dawn. I started to question myself, my instincts. I felt like a radio tuned in just one notch away from my station. I could hear, but not clearly. Wandering away from home a bit, starting to feel helpless, ridiculous, I looked down and on the side of the road I saw it- the book lying there looking at me. *The Color Purple.*

"OK," I shouted to the sky. "I get it but I don't get it!"

Yes, any onlooker would have thought I'd surely lost it and lost it for good. But at that point, with the media long gone, I could not have cared less *what* anyone thought. That was one of the biggest blessings IN the tornado. It was the first time in a long time – maybe in my LIFE – I didn't care what people thought.

"You have to help me!!!!" my voice echoed out.

Purple. Purple. Keep going.

I chugged along from one thing to the next: the random purple flip-flop, the purple suitcase holding someone else's suit coat – but nothing of ours.

"I'm lost!" I cried out.

I whipped the dirt, sawdust and sweat from my brow, and my eyes focused in on the tiniest slip of paper embedded in the bark of the tree before me. It was not even a page, not really a piece of a page of a book. It was a speck, a thumb nail, a tick tack. I leaned in to see what it said.

"By the lake" it read. By the lake. By the lake?

And then I remembered the duck pond about a half-block away, on the grounds of the high school.

"By the LAKE!" I shouted.

With new wind in my sails I booked a beeline to the water's edge where it sat in the weeds like a kid who'd been waiting too long to be picked up from school. My dad's computer! Dad's computer! God, I don't know exactly *who* you are, but I know for sure *that* you are! I thought. Thank you for guiding me! Thank you, whoever you are. Thank you! Thank you that you are with me. Thank you!

Back at the hotel that night we cleaned up, getting the glass and filth out from under our nails and trying to push it out of our heads with beers and laughter. The cousins were starting to arrive and the aunties too. It was to be a "good Irish wake." I caught a glimpse of myself in the mirror. Fried hair, dark circles, hollow cheeks. You'd think I was a junkie.

Don't you think it's strange the way things get all mashed up in really urgent times? Like when a woman delivers a baby and they are shoving a zillion pieces of paper in *her* face as she's seeing her *infant's* face for the first time? There sure is a lot of paper pushing involved with birthing and dying.

That night we signed insurance papers and signed on an attorney since my parents died without a will. We signed banking stuff and signed away the rights to the Amway Empire that was ours for the building. But with the patent and the computer and the contacts, we decided that we should keep Dad's company going.

The question was who was going to run it. Ryan was still in school. I was up to my eyeballs with work and mommy-ing. Mark was up to *his* eyeballs with his big time corporate gig. But Tim was free and so he became head of the brand new Cook Legacy. We signed the paperwork and stopped to grab a bite to eat.

Church people so rock at bringing in food. If there's one thing that the church gets right, aside from confessing Jesus as Lord and Savior, it's the food. Now, it's not always as healthy as it should be, but it's right there when it should be almost all the time.

The good church people had hooked us *up*. There was lasagna and baked chicken. There were pizzas and salad and tons and tons of cookies and cakes. As I surveyed the display, I wondered why I should choose something healthy. Why eat the celery and salad when I could just up and die in a tornado any minute? Healthy eating is a hopeful thing. It believes in a future.

"Go for the chocolate," I heard Mom say.

Wow. It was *still* going on. I swear I heard her. How weird, I thought, and reached out and grabbed a slice of triple chocolate layer cake.

"Mmmmmmm," I said as Ryan grabbed the crook of my elbow and pulled me away.

"We have to go plan the funeral, Sis," he said and we shuffled down the artificially homey hotel hallways to a conference room where the team from church was waiting around round plastic tables.

"We are so sorry for your loss," said the deacon who handled funeral planning. "Your mom and dad were great people." He seemed to mean it.

"Thank you," I said by rote.

"Did you have any ideas on music? Here's a song list to choose from."

Ryan and I scanned the list: On Eagles Wings, Be Not Afraid, Ave Maria.

I thought of every organ-driven, followed by luncheon, old person funeral I'd ever attended.

"Do you have anything up tempo?" I said.

"Pardon me?" the deacon said.

"Anything up tempo. Ya know… peppy? With a beat? Like "When the Saints Go Marching In? Can we do that?" I looked at Ryan. "Dad I'm sure at some point said that's what he wanted. With a New Orleans brass band. I don't suppose we can bring in a New Orleans brass band, with umbrellas and everything, cuz Dad would just love that."

"Yeah, yeah," Ryan said. "He totally said that. I remember that, too."

The deacon and his team shot each other disapproving looks, clearly doing their best to politely shut us down and redirect us to something more appropriate.

"No, you cannot bring in a New Orleans brass band. Our team will be playing and singing and they are very talented musicians with beautiful voices."

Ryan and I shot each other our own disapproving looks but knew that we'd never bridge the gap with this well-meaning team.

"Aren't they cute at this age, Bud?" I said to my brother, too tired to maintain proper filters.

"I'm sure they are," Ryan said to the deacon. "That will be fine. One question: is that African American man who sang the solo at Christmas going to be singing at the funeral?"

"Yeah," I said, "they LOVED him! They called him ABG – Awesome Black Guy! Is ABG gonna sing at the funeral?"

Crossing his arms and learning back in his chair, the deacon said, "Yes, Darrel will be singing."

"Can he sing 'When the Saints Go Marching In?'"

"Sure." He agreed, like a sandcastle that had been hit by a wave.

With that bit of awesome in place, and the rest of the details filled in, we hit the hay and tried to sleep. I was so tired that sleep was almost impossible. My skin was itchy. My face felt like it was growing zillions of little bumps and so I just laid still and focused on my breath until at some point, I drifted off.

I was hoping for dreams that night. Maybe Mom and Dad would come to visit me.

Maybe I could still see them when I dreamt. Maybe I'd get a God dream with information that I'd need, like why this happened. Maybe one of Lorna's angels would show up at the foot of my bed and tell me not to be afraid. As it turned out though, I didn't dream. I barely slept.

So, it was much coffee in the morning and then off to the funeral home. It doesn't matter how cozy they try to make them, funeral homes still stink like death and Kleenex and mint and always freak me out. The dear people of Tufts Schildmeyer Funeral Home were donating everything to our family, again downright proof of the goodness of mankind. As we sat down at the heavy wood table, I felt like a five year old in the giant winged back chair. I felt like I needed to sit on a phone book. I was shrinking like an old woman or an apple doll and I hoped it would continue until I simply disappeared. I searched the heavy table for a little bottle like Alice finds in Alice in Wonderland, *Drink me,* so I could fall through the rabbit hole and grow so giant I could stomp the creepy place to dust.

The funeral director entered in his customary grey suit. He was a round man with a kind face.

"I'm so sorry for your loss," he said.

"Thank you," I said. "Thank you for your kindness."

He pulled out a tiny yellow envelope and poured it out on the table. It was mom's rings. Her opal, the one she'd tried to give me just days before, the one I said I'd have one day, was perfect, not a nick to be found. Her wedding ring was crushed, diamond missing. That was when I knew for sure it was true. They were dead. It was them. No one had picked the wrong people. It wasn't a mistake. They would not show up at Kmart in Kalamazoo like Elvis one day. Lee and Jacque Cook died April 9, 1999.

A giant piece of me walked right downstairs and got embalmed right then. That piece was named Hope.

I was grateful that they died together. You see these couples, maybe you're one of them, who lose their love and then have to live on? They wander through their days, so often more bound up than the prisoners who emptied my basement, serving out their lives instead of living them. Mom and Dad certainly did not live perfectly, but at least they lived fully and together completely from beginning to end. They lived.

The morning of the funeral, I woke early. I knew it would take forever to make myself presentable and I wanted to look pretty for my parents. Funny how after your loved ones are gone, you still want to make them proud. I pulled off the covers and fumbled to tear open that nasty hotel coffee pod when I caught the first look at myself in the mirror.

"What the…?" I said as I walked over to the sink and clicked on the light. My hair was grey, or at least it *looked* grey. Every single last hair on my head had split in my sleep – big-time split ends. My split ends had split ends. I had split ends, split middles, split tops. It was a mess. There was no solving this problem. I called my friend Christa Zielke.

Christa was and is my right hand girl in Cinci. I've known her since I was 23 and she was 15. She also happens to be fabulous with all things beauty, even though she's a total jock, which is why she's so insanely cool.

I told her about my hair and she said she'd be right over.

Surveying the damage, we agreed that it all needed to be cut off and that there was no time for that right now. Christa gently, lovingly twisted my hair back in little dainty rows as I sat and wept and drank coffee.

When I tried putting on make-up, my tears washed it off. I couldn't stop. We agreed make-up was pointless and I slapped on some powder and gloss. She gave me her sunglasses and we were out the door.

"You look like Jackie Kennedy," she said. "Or Yoko. You look great."

The funeral was packed out. People had come from all over the country to bid farewell to my folks. The fatherly funeral director greeted us as the big glass doors swung open to the business inside. It was amazing. It was the opposite of "Eleanor Rigby." It was a testimony. My uncle's college buddies, my brother's youth group and lacrosse team, my buds from the D, my radio friends with their leather jackets and pony tails, *everyone* was there. What a huge difference that made. Somebody should share a business where you can hire funeral fillers like they do at the Oscars when someone has to pee. Funeral Fillers! No? You're right. Not every idea can be a winner. These people brought comfort because they were *our* people; proof that we were not alone, on that day we weren't. It was the closest to good that I could feel.

I stood in the front row. A giant picture of Mom and Dad smiling and waving good-bye was projected above the modern glass altar. It was taken at our last family reunion just last summer at my Aunty Mickey's house. Who would have known?

I just stood there, waiting and waiting for something supernatural to occur—for a voice, a message, a vision to help me understand why they were gone. I can only say I could feel them with me. It felt like a warm touch on my shoulder. That's it. It was like my open channel was closing just like a casket. I missed them.

And I missed my daughter. She wasn't with me that day. Her dad and I had decided it was best to keep her home. I think I agreed to it because I didn't really know for sure that I could keep it together and I didn't have a solid back up plan for who could take care of Alex if I unraveled. I definitely did not want to see my ex, let alone have him stand by me that day. Standing beside someone in her time of loss, I thought, was a privilege reserved for people who loved you and just a year before he'd confessed that was not the case. Some part of me didn't want to burden people with taking care of a toddler, not realizing then that helping people in times of need is a blessing, not a burden. But Alex was so little and had been through so much, I did not want to traumatize her, either. It was a tough call. I hope it was the right one.

They read the Scriptures and ABG rocked it. The priest sprinkled the caskets with holy water, we rolled them out to a big line of cameras.

"Do you have anything you'd like to say?" a young gun reporter asked.

I shook my head no as Ryan said, "Yes. I'd like to say something; I'd like to say how loving and merciful our God is. Our mom and dad loved each other. They would never want to live without each other and he took them together. What a gracious God. That's all. Thanks, guys." Ryan said, sliding on his shades. Oh, how I wish I would have known Jesus then. To *know* all things are used for the good. I didn't know that. It felt like chaos.

Yet even still, God strengthened me and I got the distinct privilege of experiencing Scripture before I even knew it was Scripture. I knew at least that He was at hand and He *did* draw near to the broken-hearted.

It was starting to rain when we got to the cemetery. The service was quick. The priest said something about, "We are dust and to dust we shall return." and with a conductor-like sign of the cross my parents were lowered into the donated plots while we sang *Amazing Grace.*

It was finished.

CHAPTER 4

THE GREAT ESCAPE

Lord you say "be still and know that I am God." I confess that the
business of life has me enticed enough that I have trouble being still.
Forgive me and show me how.

B ereavement, from the Middle English term *bereave,* means *to leave*
someone alone and desolate, especially by death. Or the archaic usage:
to take something valuable or necessary, especially by force.

The company gave me two weeks bereavement, one for mom and
one for dad. My boss said he had to go to bat for me to even get that.
Corporate wanted to give me one week until he explained the situation and they agreed to the two. I thought that was generous.

Now, my two weeks bereavement was 100% bolstered up by my
amazing group of friends, who happened to be Jewish. So, Alex and I
were grafted into the tree and they went all Shiva on us.

The tradition in Jewish households is to do what's called *Sitting*
Shiva. There's the first day after the funeral where they do almost
exactly what our Irish Catholic family did. They eat, they drink, they

sit with the grieving and they tell stories. They have a unique cleanliness ritual, too. For example, when you leave the cemetery to go to a Jewish home to nosh and talk about what a mensch the dearly departed was, you wash your hands. There is a pitcher of water at the front door of the home where people gather and you are asked to wash the "death off" before you enter. Upon entrance, you'll find all the mirrors in the home covered. It's a genius idea if you ask me! WHO wants to look at the most fried version of themselves in the mirror? Who?

For days, I think it's a week, maybe 10 days, someone comes with food and stays with the bereaved. They just hang out. They sit... Shiva... and that's exactly what my friends did for Alexandra and me. Every *day*, one of them came over.

My friend Julie, a marathoner fabulous corporate fashionista came with carry-out one day. "Girls, I brought falafel...it's good for the soul. Alex, have you ever had falafel?"

Alex shook her head and her pigtails bounced back and forth.

"No? Well isn't this exciting! Aunty Julie gets to be here for your first falafel! Take a big bite! MMMM....what do you think?"

"Yum! I love it!" Alex said, wiping tahini sauce off her chubby cheeks.

"How you doing, girl?" Julie whispered to me.

I just smiled and sighed and shook my head.

"You got out of bed today. Right?" she said. "You're right here on the couch with me. Right?"

I nodded.

"Then it's a good day. Good job."

Julie called and asked me that question every day for a month. "Did you get out of bed today?"

"Yes."

"Then it's a good day. Good job."

She and my friends, Brett and Deb and Phil and Jason all took turns checking in on me, always bringing dinner and always staying for a sit.

It was amazing. They were not on some committee at church where they signed on to make a hot dish for babies and dead folk. They were not obliged to and yet they did. They didn't do it to earn points to get into heaven or for what I may do for them in return. They just organically extended love and grace, help and support. They rocked, solid rocked. They did grief brilliantly and I am forever grateful.

The way my friends handled me was positively tribal. They were like Marines. They had a man down and they would not leave me or Alexandra to bleed out in the field.

Alexandra seemed really fine. She wasn't regressing or acting out, at least not that her teachers, grandparents, dad or I could discern. But she had a big problem, and it was me. I was a wreck. I could barely breathe. I was having trouble defining the edges of reality.

I was having a hard time discerning between Earth and Oz. I wanted so badly to stay connected to my parents, I spent almost all the time that I wasn't working, grocery shopping or picking up Alex in seated meditation just trying to get out of my body.

I could barely function. Could I say I was hopeful? Not really. I had no idea what this life was about, but I sure spent a lot of time pondering that question. I was what the Christians called a seeker and boy, did I seek. Partly because I was really interested in understanding God, who I DID think loved me, but at the same time did not seem to care about me at all. I was not aware of a sovereign God. I did not know a God who had reconciled everything. I had no idea my debt was paid...or Mom's or Dad's, for that matter. I didn't know if they'd been *good enough*. I knew for sure that I wasn't and I also believed that it was up to me – and everyone else – to earn my way into heaven. But I did know this: life on Earth was awful.

It was mean and cruel and ugly and I didn't want to watch another evening newscast and pretend that the world was just ducky. It wasn't and I wanted out. I was tipping on the edge of suicidal.

My poor therapist, Laura, had a whole new adventure on her hands. She was a late twenty-something rock star of a counselor. I had been seeing Laura for months already, since John left. I was so angry at that time. I was viciously, violently angry. Believe me when I tell you, there was a lot of kick boxing going on. I worked through that with Laura and was really feeling quite fabulous again when the tornado hit. Suddenly, Laura was faced with a science experiment. Our first, post-tornado conversation went something like this:

How are you feeling, Shannyn?

Silence

Can you tell how you are feeling?

Nod.

Can you put words on it?

Head shake.

Do you want to talk today?

Nod…silence.

Long silence.

OK.

Silence.

Can you talk today?

Another head shake.

I was barely there. I was on life support. I was animated flesh with tear ducts.

All I could do when I got into the safety of her room was cry and cry and cry.

I had no idea where all that water came from. It was like when you have a baby and your water breaks and you think, *how can this all be in me? When will it stop?* It's crazy how many tears you can cry. I was a faucet…a silent one. I just wept and wept without making a sound, my gut wrenching, my brow furrowed down so hard I thought it may never release, which in fact it did not.

Laura just sat there quietly. I loved her for not trying to do anything. She just witnessed it and she wasn't shocked or afraid of me. There was nothing at all that I could ever say to Laura that would shock her. She wasn't afraid of me even when I was afraid of me.

Finally, I tried to get out a word, just to see if my voice would work.

"I am so sad. I am so, so sad. I'm sad. I feel sad and mad and scared and alone.

And I hear a screaming in my head and all the buildings look like they're blown over and I think I may be going crazy."

"OK," she said. "Good."

And then we just sat there for most of the rest of the hour.

"Do you feel suicidal at all?" she'd say.

"A little. Not like I'm gonna do it, but I can see why people do."

She reached down and pulled some mints from her purse and then popping a tic-tac in her mouth replied, "Well, there are medications, not for the long term, but for now. That may help you if you'd like to talk about that option."

"No, I don't think I need to do that."

"OK. Do you know what you *do* need right now?"

"I need my mom," I said. My face clenched up again and caught the tears which never stopped into channels down my cheeks and chin and throat and chest and lap.

"What do you want to do today? If you could do anything this afternoon...what would you do?"

"I'd go home and get Alex and get on a plane and fly to the ocean and stay on the beach for as long as we wanted....months...years. We would just lie on the beach and listen to the ocean and soak in the sun and build castles until the sun set and then we'd do it all over again. I would run. I would run to the ocean...to someplace warm where they don't have tornadoes."

And I wept more, even as I thought, I have to pull it together. This hour's almost over. Her next client is in the lobby, Shannyn. Breathe. You have to drive soon. You have to act OK again.

"That sounds nice." Laura nodded and took notes. "Does anything help?" she said.

"Chocolate helps."

She laughed.

"And meditation."

The bell went "ding" and our time was up.

We doubled our meetings to twice a week, filled in our calendars. I wiped off my face, took a deep breath and oozed out of her office to my car.

Counting Crows' *The Long December* played on the radio of my silver Civic as I pulled out of the lot and into the five o'clock traffic. The dreadlocked singer whined his lyric: *It's been a long December but there's reason to believe maybe this year will be better than the last.* Is there, I thought? Is there reason to believe that? "Well IS THERE?" I cried aloud? "I DON'T SEE IT, GOD!" I weaved through the Detroit rush hour bustle of busy, fabulous people with busy fabulous lives to meet with Alex and LaJeana.

LaJeana Kennedy. Let me tell you, *there* is a woman of God. She is nothing if not a channel of the Divine. When she walked through her valley of death, losing her beautiful Sammy, she did what I was doing. She went deep, deep into a cave and communed with the Spirit and emerged all scarred up. Jeanie had had several years to grieve and rebound and heal, and she'd even moved on to adopting her son, Isaiah. Jeanie was proof to me that I could survive. She lived to tell the tale and that gave me hope...not so much that I *would* survive, but that I *could,* that it was even a possibility.

Pulling into the drive, I checked my face in the mirror. I looked like a shriveled balloon. With powder and lip gloss, I put on my game face and went in to see the ladies.

Jeanie greeted me with, "How was your day, Honey?" and then announced my arrival to Alex. "Hey," I said with maybe my first smile of the day as Alex came bounding down the hallway in a tutu and fairy wings.

"Look at my WAND, Mommy!" she cried. "Jeanie got it for me!"

"It's sooooo pretty! Does it work?" I say. "Let's try it out! House, be clean!" I took the wand and gave it a snap. "Hum…it must be broken. Dinner! Be done! Nope. You try it, Alex."

"Dinner! Be pizza!" She squeezed her big blue eyes shut and waved with all her fairy princess might. Then daring to peek and see if pizza had not, in fact, materialized, she shrugged her wings and said, "I must be sleepy."

She grabbed her blanky to snuggle in bed.

Alex had taken to sucking her thumb and was super attached to "blanky." I could understand. I wanted to suck my thumb, too.

LaJeana gave me the day's report while she grabbed her bags and put the toys back in their basket. "It's been a busy day. We went to the park and had a picnic and played on everything. I mean every-thing, girl." Reaching into her purse, she pulled out Alex's favorite doll. "She sure does love this Betty Spaghetti all right! Isaiah, c'mon bud, let's go."

Isaiah, a giant one-year-old, came trucking down the hall from Alex's room in overalls and work boots. Jeannie scooped him up in her arms and we had a group hug. "Well good bye, honey. I'll see you tomorrow." She pressed her sweaty cheek to mine and whispered, "It'll be all right, honey." And she was gone.

The house…it got so quiet.

I sat there on the floor of the tiny front room. To my right was the dining room table where we had just shared our last supper as a family. I wonder, I thought, if their fingerprints are on my table. I should have it dusted. Then I could press them on paper and save them forever.

I let out a cry. It was that sound, you know the one that soldiers make when they lay groaning in the trenches. It was that sharp, deep moan that sounds like an emergency siren from the soul, from the earth itself. I'd only made that sound one other time. It was when John told me he was leaving. When he said, "I never loved you. I've been acting the whole time. I can't do it anymore. I'm sorry, Shannyn. I do not love you. How can I make you understand? It's over. I'm leaving you. That's what's going on here."

I'd begged him to understand, to give it a chance, to wait—that this feeling would blow over and in a month, or a year or a *day*, he would say "Thank God I didn't leave."

But he said, "We've been through this before. It is over, Shannyn. I can't do this. I DON'T LOVE YOU! I NEVER HAVE. I'M SORRY. IT'S OVER."

My entire world came crashing off a cliff and everything I ever believed or dreamed of shattered in a zillion pieces. In one little turn of a hinge, I became a single mom. I made that noise then. It was probably 4 am and we were still fighting and I was too tired to fight any more and I curled into the fetal position with my back to the outstretched John and made that noise. "Ahhhhhh......" "Ahhhhhh...." "I'm wounded" I said. "I'm wounded." And I cried until the sun came up and John was leaving and kissing our baby good-bye.

As he shut the door he simply said, "Good-bye, Shannyn. I'm sorry."

That was the noise that came out of me as soon as Jeanie left too.

"Where are you?" I cried out loud. "Help me. I need help."

I cried for an hour until Alex got out of bed and floated into my room. She sat at my feet sucking her thumb and rubbing her nose with the silky edge of her blanky.

"Are you OK, mommy?" she said.

"Yes, I'm OK baby," I told her. "Mommy's just sad. I miss Grandma and Grandpa. But I'm OK and you're OK and we're OK. OK?"

"OK, mommy. Can we order pizza?"

"Yep. That's OK, too. I guess we're gonna have to since the wand is broken," I said, bopping her little nose. "And then we'll pack our suitcase, Pumpkin. We're going to go and visit the ocean!"

In one call to my boss and a couple of clicks on Priceline, we were California bound. I know it's cliché. I couldn't help it. John's family was still treating me and Alex like one of their own, holding out hope for reconciliation. His aunt had a vacant condo near the beach and generously offered it to us rent free. So San Diego it was.

Aunt Jane: organizational queen, welcomed us into the open expanse of her Cali condo with a giant pearly smile.

"Here is your new home, ladies!"

A jasmine breeze blew through. Her pantry looked like the Pinterest police had just inspected it. It was stocked with staples in neatly labeled wicker baskets, all the pantry basics in alphabetical order: apples in the basket on the left, then bananas and Cliff bars. I hoped that this time would be like a reset button. You know, like when rich people go away to the spa for a month of yoga and salad, massages and herbal tea wraps, coming back thin, refreshed and looking 10 years younger? I was hoping for the free, staying at your Aunty-out-law's version of that.

"See, P for pancake mix, Alex," Aunt Jane said. She lifted a basket. "Pancake mix gets it very own basket, because it's *so* messy. Yucky mess." She wiped the shelf and then set the basket down. The place was clean. Clean, clean, clean. Like a white out.

"Yuck. Mess," Alex repeated dusting her little hands.

We…are in trouble, I thought, as I do not seem to be gifted with keeping things surgically clean.

"Jane, thank you so much for letting us come out and stay and for the food. Can I pay you for that?"

"Oh, heavens no," Jane said, "I wouldn't dream of it. I'm just grateful that we can. I want you to feel at home. Treat this like your home while you're here. She swept around the corner of the lofty space and swung a door open, "This is your room, Alexandra! Look! You have your very own bathroom and two beds!"

I could hear the ocean outside, and people laughing.

"Yeah! For bouncing," said Alex with a cheer. My jaw clenched as I braced for the impact of Jane's rebuke.

"Yes! For bouncing. And your mom's room is right around the corner. See!"

My room was small and white…of course. It had a dresser, a bed and a lovely bedside table with a potted violet and a framed black and white photo of an old wrinkled turban-wearing Indian man.

"Who's that?" I asked.

"Oh, that's Paramahansa Yogananda. His ashram and gardens are right around the corner from here. You should go! It's the most beautiful place in the world. You'll see. The dolphins are right there. It's free! The hours are posted on the gate."

"Can you walk there?" I said, already wishing I'd rented a car.

"Oh yes. It's literally right around the corner from here. If you go down the hill and curve to the right, you'll see a big metal gate on the left. It'll say SRF garden. The hours will be there. There's a plaque on the gate. I think it opens at 8."

She stood perfectly still, like a tall mountain. Her eyes were shining stars-the same kind as the youth group kids.

"It stands for Self Realization Fellowship. It's a group founded by Yoganada. You'll see. There'll be monks sitting around meditating. But just make yourself at home." Aunt Jane smiled at Alex. "Don't get too loud there. The monks like it quiet and so do the fish."

Alex giggled and nodded in agreement. Jane handed me the keys and gave me a hug. "I love you," she said, "Enjoy yourself"

After a giant hug for each of us she swept out the door.

Alex and I were both beat from the day's travel and headed straight to showers and jammies. Alex clicked on the TV and snuggled up in my bed with a big bowl of green grapes.

"Um, those look yummy," I said. "I'm gonna go get some tea. Be right back." As I walked down the long white hallway to the alphabetical kitchen two things were happening in my head. One was a keen awareness of the fact that I was starting to forget the details of the

Shannyn Caldwell

tornado…that my mind was actively blocking my access to the information and it worried me.

The other was the idea of living in a sterile white condo with a wee one and trying to keep it clean. Frankly, the latter worried me more. To say that people who aren't saved don't spend a lot of time in prayer is not true. Anyone – I mean anyone – who's been in a rented white room with a three year old has prayed. Well …prayed and hidden the ketchup.

Tea…tea…I thought, passing coffee. Oh yes…if there's tea here, it's bound to be under T…but nope. No big deal…we'd walk to the grocery store in the morning, or after we visited that garden…and then I saw it, Tea…in the J basket, for Jasmine…right next to the jelly…grape jelly, which I also hid.

"Alex," I called to her, "have you ever tried peanut butter marshmallow cream sandwiches? *No?* Well, we'll be getting some marshmallow cream at the store tomorrow, fluffy white marshmallow cream, cream soup, and some white tea…and bleach!"

The next morning I woke to a warm breeze carrying the smell of the jasmine outside the window and marrying it to the jasmine in the cup on my nightstand. Stretching my arms and legs and looking to my side I saw Yoganada there in the picture. I wondered if there was something to this man, this garden, this Self Realization Fellowship. It kind of sounded California wishy-washy, but hey, we were in California, after all. May as well catch the wave!

So I woke my sleeping princess and brushed out her long brown hair. We quickly got dressed in WAY fewer clothes than we would have to wear back home in the April cold, popped a couple Cliff Bars, water and fruit into my backpack and, armed with brand new notebooks and super sharp pencils, we were off.

Jane was right, the garden was easy to find, just down the palm lined hill and to the right, marked with elegant iron filigree gates. Self-Realization Fellowship, a lapis blue plaque read. Open to the public.

"You wanna open the gate?" I asked the wide eyed Alex. "Go ahead!"

"OK." And with the tiniest push, they swung gently open.

It was like Disney. It was like Eden. It was the Celestine Prophecy meets Narnia without the unicorns. It was beautiful. It was Willy Wonka's Chocolate Factory amazing without the cream filled mushrooms and gummy bear flowers.

A middle aged man sat silently under a pink blooming tree, legs crossed under saffron robes, meditating. At his feet stretched a bubbling koi pond being freshly fed by a trickle of water coming down the hill of grey stacked stone. Jasmine was everywhere and magnolia and geranium. They were huge and their perfume was so strong in the air that if a woman had sprayed it on, her co-workers would complain. My eyes were on overload from all the beauty. What a treasure it was to allow something lovely to pass my retina for a change.

Alex and I became instantly still…quiet. It was a taste of peace and I wanted more. Alex and I floated up tree-lined stone stairs, stopping to smell baskets of flowers which hung from branches along the path, leading eventually to a cliff which overlooked the Pacific Ocean.

"Look honey, there it is!" I said, taking little Alex by the hand. "It's the ocean! Listen, do you hear it?"

Squinting her eyes, she trained her ear and listened. "YES! I hear it!"

"Do you smell it, sweetie?"

With a deep inhale and a big smile she said, "I smell salty…fishhh!"

"Yep, that's it all right! Let's sit down and be quiet for a while and see how much we can see and hear and smell and taste when we are perfectly quiet."

"What about touch, Mommy?"

"Good question, honey bear. What about touch. Well...let's see what we touch when we just sit still."

"Or what touches us, right Mommy?"

"Yes, baby. Or what touches us."

Alex had and still has an uncanny ability to be still. A trait I lack. *Still* is not my natural behavior. I've been nervous my whole life. Some have suggested that it has something to do with being born prematurely. I was born very early. I weighed less than a pound and all of me fit into the palm of my grandpa's hand. My mom was 5 months pregnant when I was born. The nurses and doctors at Wright Pat AFB wouldn't let my mom hold me. They told her I was "going to die anyway and she shouldn't bond with me." That if I did live I'd be so mentally retarded that she'd wish I'd died. It was the next day before my mom dragged herself using the IV as a walker and demanded they let her hold me.

I do think I have a memory from that time. You never really *know* if it's a memory or just your imagination, but I think I remember being in an incubator and I was so, so weak. I think I remember a silver cord, like an umbilical cord, and it connected me to heaven and I was trying like crazy to climb up it and get out of here and back to there, but I was too weak. I couldn't do it. I gave up. I didn't die. I lived. I'm here to tell the tale, by God's grace. Some suggest that's why I've always had an undercurrent of nervousness. If so, guess what? He can heal that, too, in His perfect time. This time, however, I joined Alex in her stillness and traced the sound of the ocean back to my breath.

I'd learned a little about meditation in acting school. An acting professor named Mark Olson taught me how to meditate. I knew how to begin...drawing my shoulder blades on my back, tucking them in like wings, lifting my heart to the warm sun...inhale peace, exhale confusion, I'd think. Inhale, soften your brow, exhale, and relax your jaw. Inhale peace, exhale confusion. I didn't yet have the Holy Spirit to take me by the hand to the throne room, but I did have the Lord our Father calling out to me and when I sought Him with all my heart

He did exactly what He promises in His Word He will do: "If you seek me with all of your heart, I will be found by you." (Jeremiah 29:13)

Inhale peace…peace ascended on us both. At one point, I thought, *how long have we been here? Has it been an hour? Is it lunchtime?* Alex, quiet as a mouse in her baby blue hoodie, was tucked into the beat of her own heart. I dove back into my breath.

Inhale, lifting up through the crown of my head. Exhale, tucking my tailbone and rooting through my sitz bones. Inhale and open your heart, Shannyn. Open your heart.

I'm scared to open my heart, I thought. God, my heart is broken. It is broken. It's jelly, not muscle. It's over. I'm broken. I'm lost.

Inhale peace…don't follow the wave of fear, Shannyn. Come back home, Shannyn. Inhale peace. Exhale confusion. Inhale, soften your brow. Exhale, relax your jaw. Inhale, just inhale, slowly, evenly into every corner of your lungs…peace. Exhale, slowly exhale washing the fear out of every cell. Be still. Let go. Let God…whatever that is. Trust.

I softened and offered up thoughts like burnt offerings to the Lord. "I need help." Then inhale and exhale "I'll be your help." said the still small voice. "Who will love me?" I cried out. "I will love you and you will love me." "Mom! Dad! Where ARE YOU?" Inhale, fill your lungs as the salty air swept me clean I wonder again…Am I awake? What time is it?

Now it had been an hour or so. Alex had gotten out the Leap Pad from the backpack and was playing quietly, her long hair covering all of her face and most of her tiny body.

Jasmine perfumed everything, salt and jasmine and the sound of the ocean. Life is good, I thought. At least there is good in it. At least there is some good.

I'd have to focus on that. For her sake, we would focus on that. Inhale, draw your shoulder blades on your back. Open your heart. Exhale, soften your jaw. Soften your brow.

I whispered to Alex, "Ya hungry, baby? Want a piece of fruit?"

"Um, no thank you."

"Here, drink some water." I handed her the bottle and opened up a Cliff bar for myself.

Eating a peanut butter Cliff bar now takes me right back to that moment. If I have a water bottle, it's even stronger. The mind is wild like that. When I eat one today, I smell jasmine, feel fresh faced, free and well...and like crying. I don't eat peanut butter Cliff bars much, for just that reason, which is a bummer, because they're the bomb.

As we sat now hip to hip on the lovely cement bench watching the ocean...the surfers in the distance and then the dolphins coming out to play alongside . . . I thought, there is beauty. There is goodness. Focus on that. Focus on sharing that with Alex.

"Look Alex!" I cried out. "Do you see the dolphin? See it over there?"

She traced my outstretched finger to its end just as a dolphin, as if on cue, leapt straight in the air and arched back with a giant splash.

"WOW!" she said, and then we sat silently watching, sipping our water and drinking it all in.

That is exactly what we did, day after day for almost a month and at night, I'd write every single thing that I could remember in case I ever wanted to know what had happened. I could feel my brain covering up the crime scene that was my memory. I wrote it down because I knew I was actively and aggressively forgetting things. Don't get me wrong, there are plenty of things I'd love to forget in my life, but I just would love to have control over *which* things they were. I didn't seem to have a choice. And while I wrote, Alex watched Power Puff girls making the world safe...before bed time.

Meditation was fast becoming my favorite secret hiding place-my flying dream, awake. If I could stay up above it all, see it from the eagle's eye view, maybe it could make sense. I would sit silently listening to my breath or listening to the scream. The scream in the back of my head began on the ground of the house...when I reached down and found Mom's coat. The scream came with the taste of tornado dirt and the smell of cigarettes and Estee Lauder.

It never stopped. I'd wake and make coffee to the sound of the scream. I'd shower, cook, brush Alex's hair, smoke a cigarette, write it all out, mediate at the garden, and lay my body down to the sound of the scream. It was always, always there…a single female voice screaming a high pitched wail at the top of her lungs. It was like a TV that I couldn't shut off. Sometimes I'd just sit and listen to her scream. I'd picture her in the middle of a field…all black and white and the camera far away at first, then zooming in and zooming round and round getting closer and closer still until it landed at last in her mouth and disappeared into the blackness of her throat. I'd imagine her vocal chords.

Yet even with the ocean, the garden, the voice of the Lord, a perfect daughter, a place to stay for free, a brother who loved me…I still heard the scream and wanted to punch something so hard it shattered to bits. I wanted to punch and punch and punch and kick and yell and scream right along with that girl in my head. I was livid. I was lost.

Thankfully, I was also not alone. Ryan had decided he was in dire need of a trip to the beach as well and so was meeting us and staying for the last week of the month.

Seeing Ryan was the greatest. It was proof that my world was still out there and that I had not in fact fallen into a Holodeck called California.

We spent most of our time on the beach. Ryan didn't want to talk much. Mostly he liked to run…and look at girls. I remember thinking, hum…this guy is a Christian and he's checking out girls on the beach. I was a little judgmental about that. I held Christians to an impossibly high standard. One I'm super glad I don't have to live up to today. He and I both take that experience into account today as we strive to walk out a witness.

The one thing Ryan insisted on while he was there was that we try what he called *The Disney Solution*. Disney, gotta love it right? Most magical place on earth, right? Sure, right. Love it. Also wish it was free because nothing crashes through a mouse house faster than no cash. If it was truly a magic kingdom, it would be free.

Did we have a blast? You bet. Did we ride the rides, watch the parades, the concerts, play with Merlin and try to pull the sword out of the rock? You know we did. Spinning Tea Cups, drag racing, haunted-mansioning it up with a back pack of water and Cliff bars and apples, until the sun was way down. Alex was bent over from exhaustion and sleeping with dirty feet in sandals resting inside her stroller. I took my sweater from around my waist and covered her up.

"You ready to go home, Buddy?" I said to my brother.

"Naw. I thought we'd see if we could hide out in here and spend the night. Just see how long we could hide, ya know? I think we could do a day, for sure. Then we'd have to jack a dude for his suite or something."

We laughed.

"Naw. Let's go," I said.

We were healing. We were moving on. We were actually having fun and making good new memories. We didn't like that our lives were changing. We didn't choose it or want it. But there it was and it was a little bit good. We had each other.

Ryan never tried to evangelize me with words. He sat around and read his Bible a lot. He didn't want to go to the bar with me when I wanted to go. Instead he offered to watch Alex so I could go, an offer I totally took him up on most nights. Again, had I been a follower of Christ at the time, I likely would have wanted to stay home. I didn't know Him and without Him nothing made sense at all. The world was meaningless, brutal, unjust, unkind, unforgiving and worst of all, random. I didn't rest in anything and so I didn't rest.

I went to the bar to hear music. I danced. I flirted. I smoked cigarettes and hooked up with beach boys. Yet absolutely nothing ever brought peace and it was almost time to wind up the trip and go back home to work again. I did not know how I was ever going to be able to do it. I was jealous of childless people who flipped out because they could just decide they wanted to be called Moonshadow and drink wheatgrass juice and chill in robes in a garden all day and do service to the ashram and never ever say another word in their life if they didn't want to.

I wanted to take a vow of silence. I wanted out. I wasn't suicidal. I wasn't even depressed. I was just done with life. With the body, the bills, the husbands who leave. But, Alex... she pulled me through. That little girl saved my life a million times.

"Do you think you can do it?" I asked my bro over breakfast near the end of our stay. "Go back to school and finish up?" I looked him deliberately in the eye to look for the truth.

"Yeah. Yeah. I think." He looked down, peeling the wrapper off his bottle of o.j. "I mean it's paid for and I have my guys to room with. I should be good. You good with work...I mean going back?"

"I think so. I hope so. If I start crashing, I'll just amp up my therapy." I really did think I could at least try to pull it off, "My therapist rocks. I won't crash."

"Cool," he said, pulling the last of the wrapper off his juice and stuffing the mess back into the bottle. "So...tell me about this garden you've been hanging out in. I mean, what's the deal with it?"

"Well...it's the most beautiful place in the whole entire word, for starts. It's the SFR garden. Self-Realization Fellowship.

"Interesting." He suddenly sounded like Sherlock.

"I've only read their literature, ya know, a couple booklets, but I know they love to meditate and so do I." I looked him right in the eye again, waiting for a challenge. "I wish Christians would meditate," I added.

"Well, we do. On Scripture. That's why I read my Bible all the time. But, I'm glad that you like the garden and that it's brought some peace to you." He sounded sincere in the part about wishing me peace. He sounded, well, worried when he said he was glad I liked the garden. Almost like a dad who does not like the guy you're dating but still says, "Have fun, kids," as you close the door behind you. I think he was afraid of where this garden was taking me.

"Thanks, Bud. I love you."

"I love you, too."

"I miss Mom and Dad," I said.

"Me, too." He shook his head with a sigh and took off his baseball hat and held it to his heart. I could tell that deep inside he wanted to whip it and flip the table over. Or, perhaps I was just projecting. But no.

"Do you have support in case you, like break down or whatever?" I asked, pouring more cream into the bad coffee.

"I don't think I'm gonna break down or whatever. But if I do, yeah. I got support. I wouldn't worry though. I have yet to even cry." I was relieved to hear him acknowledge that. I didn't know if he was even aware of how shut down his emotions seemed to be.

"I know, Bud. And I cry, like all the time." Tears were even then running down my cheeks one whole month later.

"Yeah," Ryan said.

"But, Buddy, that's what I'm worried about." I said, taking his hands in mine, "That you don't cry. That you seem fine. Are you fine? I mean…are you?" I searched his eyes, his breath for clues. No sign.

"Hum…I know. I worry about that, too." Why was my brother Data from Star Trek all of a sudden? I knew he was feeling *somthing*.

"It's gotta come out, ya know. One way or another."

Just then little Alex emerged from the hall in her princess nightgown, dragging her blanky. "Yeah, Uncle Ryan," she said. "Let it out." And then she popped her thumb in her mouth. Ryan laughed like Santa and motioned for Alex to come jump up in his lap, which she did with a leap.

"Well, guys, it's a big day." I said, wiping down Alex's place mat and setting her breakfast plate out. "We have to sparkle this place up and head to home sweet home. Pop up here and have a waffle, little one. Then, let's go smell the jasmine and say good-bye to the beach. It's an airport day!"

As we descended into Detroit Metro Airport, I realized that I was still seeing flattened houses. I apparently had an architectural reprieve in California, as the homes looked so different with their adobe, tile and clay. But when my eyes hit your good old fashioned Henry Ford assembly line-looking Midwestern suburb...they all looked like heaps of debris and the girl in my head...well she just screamed.

One of the first things I wanted to do was go to breakfast at one of my very favorite Ferndale breakfast joints. If you're ever in Ferndale, say the name "Delia's" to any local and they will say "Mmmmmm" and love you forever. It was epic, brilliant breakfast and is sadly now closed. Alex was with John for the weekend and I hooked up with my buddy for a bite. There was a twenty-minute wait, so I decided to sit outside.

There was a beautiful man on the park bench out front. He had long blonde hair in a ponytail and tan skin and the deepest bright green eyes. He also had muscles for days and was wearing a green linen shirt, khaki shorts and work boots. This man was hot. I literally said a prayer right there: "Thank you, God for making men that look like that. They make the world so beautiful."

I didn't want to "make him my man." I was just grateful that there were such men in that way I'm grateful for trees and rivers and beautiful sunsets and Godiva chocolate and fluffy little kittens and the Grand Canyon and Niagara Falls. Just a "You make the world beautiful kind of way." And I thought the people in his life must be blessed.

And then he was looking at me and nodding and smiling and saying, "Hey."

"Hi," I said back.

"Cool shirt."

I was wearing a T-shirt screen printed with the painting of Tatania and the Fairies from Shakespeare's *A Midsummer Night's Dream.*

"Do you believe in fairies?" the hot man said.

"Yep. Do you?" Since when do hot men hang out and talk fairies?, I thought. *Straight* men, I mean. When do *they*?

"Sure do, but I don't think they necessarily have to be small." What? So he believes in them? I started scanning for signs of crazy, but didn't see any other than the obvious ones. No Marti Gras beads. No dog collar and black nails. No distinct body odor.

"Really. You ever seen one?" I don't know if I wanted to hear yes or no...

"Yep and it was as big as the sun."

"Wild." I wanted to hear more about this big as the sun fairy the hot guy had seen, but I thought I may ring the crazy meter for HIM, if I dug for deets. "You going to the Renaissance Festival?"

"Yeah. How'd ya know?"

"Um...fairies on the brain? Plus, you just kinda look like you're going to the Renaissance Festival. I have a friend who works out there. Any chance that if I give you a note, you can bring it to her?"

"Yeah, sure." He puffed out his chest, super-hero style, and then crossed his legs like a nerd. Who IS this guy? "I mean, if you tell me where to find her. Her name and stuff. No problem. I'll bring your note."

"Thank you so much," I said, grabbing a scrap of paper from my purse and scribbling down a note. "Her name is Dolly and she's a boot maker for Bald Mountain Boots. She's got long dark hair. Just ask for Dolly and tell her you've got a note from Shannyn...or she may call me Putter."

I passed the note to him. He tucked it into his pocket and said, "Sure thing. So, should I call you Putter?"

"Shannyn, Putter. Whatever you want. And what's your name?"

"Joseph," he said.

"Nice to meet you, Joseph." I said, in a friendly, but final way. I had no plans to let my brain drift into love land but he sure was cute. Maybe I'd let him into a daydream sometime. "Thanks for bringing Dolly my note. Give her a hug for me, OK?"

"Nice to meet you, too, Shannyn, and sure. I will." And he gave the note a kiss and popped it into his wallet.

I headed back inside as my friend was being seated. Smiling, I slid in the booth next to Christy and said, "Look at that guy. Isn't he the hottest thing ever in the world? He just kissed my note!"

"He kissed your WHAT? Which guy?" "There. With the long hair." Christy raised her perfectly arched eyebrow. I think she practiced that In the mirror, because her raised eyebrow look was Latin soap opera perfect.

"Yeah, girl. He's totally hot. You should go talk to him."

"I already talked to him."

"You should give him your number."

"No way."

"You should get his number, then. Come on! Life is short. Live it up."

"No. I'm good." I breathed deep and let it out slow. "I've already loved. I'm done with that. I have Alex and me and that's all I need. I'm really not interested. I just think he's pretty. That's all." Mercifully the waitress approached. "Hi," I said, probably too cheerfully. "I'll have coffee and the special."

"The same," Christy said, "plus throw in that hot guy at the counter for my friend here."

Our server popped her hip to the side as her pigtails bounced to the left as she bit her pencil like a milk-bone.

"Oh, Joe? Isn't he the cutest? He's a nice guy, ya know. I mean, he's a jerk like everyone, but he's a really good dude."

Christy leaned in and lowered her voice. "Is he single?"

"Stop," I said, giving her a little kick under the table, "Seriously."

"I think so. I don't think he's going with anyone right now anyway. Not that I know of."

"Thank you." Christy glared into my eyes.

"I'm done and done, Christy," I said when the waitress was gone. "I am done. You know what they say. Better to have loved and lost then never to have loved at all. Plus, I have nothing to give right now. I'm a black hole. Are you kidding? I can barely make it through eating breakfast in public. I feel like I suck the life out of everything, ya know? I feel like just being around me brings people down."

"No, that's not true," Christy said waving her hands in the air. "Not at all."

"Cuz it feels that way and I can barely handle this crowd. Everyone's so happy and I'm so not. I have like almost no energy at all. Where the heck is that coffee?"

Christy was lining up her two creams and three sugars in a perfect row with the spoon at the ready. "It's not like that. I know, coffee, right?"

"And I sure as heck can't handle a big crowd. Like there's no way I could go to the Renaissance Festival and see Dolly, and I always go. She always calls Mom when they come to town then Mom calls me. I hope he gives her the note."

"What note?"

"I gave that guy a note to give to Dolly, the note he *kissed*."

"For real?" Her already giant eyes cracked open like a double yoked egg. "He's going to deliver your note? You should give him your phone number."

"I'm not going to give him my phone number," I said, reaching for hand sanitizer.

"Do you want *me* to give him your phone number?" She grabbed the bottle and squeezed some on her hands, too.

"I'm good. I'm done. But thanks."

"Just get his number then, to make sure he gave her your note."

"If he wants my number, it's written down in the note to Dolly." I popped the bottle back in my purse.

As it turned out, Joseph delivered my note. I knew, because Dolly called me to thank me for sending a hottie to her booth. And we laughed and caught up and I told her about my mom and dad and we had a good long sisterhood cry together.

And then there was work. To be honest, I was a shell of a human at Metro Networks. I did traffic reports that sounded good. I was on time. I didn't sit and cry all day long, but I was a void…a vacuum. You ever see those pictures on Pinterest of a dog who's lying down on his soldier's grave? Yeah. That was me.

It was during a Mid-day shift at Metro, I got a call at the traffic office. As I finished my report, Lorna whispered under her breath, "Mark Thompson's on the phone for you."

"Who?" I asked, closing up my mic from a feed.

"Mark Thompson. I think he's a pretty big deal, honey. I know he used to be at WRIF (the number one rock station in Detroit) and I think he's a big wig somewhere right now. Pick it *up*!"

Mark Thompson wanted to meet and talk to me about an opening he had. And so we met and he was the smartest, coolest guy with the most amazing voice in the universe, a deep natural rock jock voice. He was 100% Native American and to make matters worse (or better) he lived on a sailboat. If that was not dreamy, I didn't know what was. And like Charlie to Charlie's Angels, he was calling Metro Networks to "take me away from all that. Now…I work for him" and became the Program Director and Afternoon Drive host of my very own radio station! They even had onsite daycare of Alex, for *free*! There was a gym onsite with free kickboxing to let it all out on my lunch hour and free yoga at the end of the day. I thought, God *must* be real, because *this* is a blessing. There's no doubt about it.

And I'd pray, too. On my way into work, I'd just pray, "Show me your will. Help me to do your will."

And so, with a dream job and a dreamy boss who was perfectly untouchable and a beautiful daughter who loved me to infinity and painted me beautiful pictures at school and watched movies with me on the couch, life really was good.

But it was hard and I still cried every night. I still heard the screaming, but I had hope. Just the tiniest little speck of hope, but somewhere I was still connecting to God and it was keeping utter despair just at bay. It's a good thing, too, because some awful things happened in that season, too.

My mentor, Steve Kay, from WWJ News Radio 950, where I did my traffic on the :08's was diagnosed with a brain tumor and died. Quickly. Suddenly. He was buried less than a month after the tornado, on my 30th birthday. He was one of the only people in the business who I knew had my back. Now I'd lost Mom and Dad and John and Steve. It was like a body count of those who had either died or bailed on me.

The list of people I could rely on through thick and thin was a thread hanging on my brother. It was really about then that I tipped over the edge of despair to suicidal. It happened in one moment, in my back yard.

I was in my filthy coveralls, working in the garden and trying like crazy to figure it all out. I was having it *out* with God. I was trying against hope as I pulled the weeds all the way down at their roots while Alex played on her swing set. "What are you trying to teach me?" I'd ask, believing that there was some lesson I needed to learn, some test to pass in order to finally be done with the beautiful, brutal cycle of life. I believed, based mostly on my environment of friends and the literature from SRF that I had to earn my way into nirvana. We all believed it, my friends and I, and we were trying. We volunteered at soup kitchens. We gave people rides to the airport. We made art and music and grew beautiful gardens. Still, I knew, I just knew that I was far from good enough and trying with all my might to be good enough brought me not even close to good enough. No matter how far down I dig, I thought as I clawed the earth and dug out dandelion roots and pulled mini tress from the ground, it will never be over. There will always be more weeds to pull. Why do I bother? It is hopeless. What's the point?

I felt that way about my hurt and anger and fear. I knew, no matter how many times I sat on my therapist's couch and talked, more weeds would pop up and eventually I would lose the battle and be over-run. I knew I couldn't make it back to normal again, but I was going to die trying.

That is a desperate place indeed. That is hopeless, and that's what I was. Hopeless. For me, being suicidal never went as far as thinking of a plan, let alone take action on following through on it. It was just a total understanding of why one would and a decision not to go there, for Alex's sake.

It was at work that November when I finally lost it. November is about the time Program Directors of radio stations do what's called "writing Christmas liners." Those are the little messages that come on between songs to connect what's going on in your life to your station. Liners like: "If you're running errands or relaxing with a good book-thanks for letting us be part of your weekend! WXYZ101!"

We strived to have insight into the lives of the listener. To put our finger on her pulse. In order to better serve a listener, you need to know what's important to them. What they need. What they're doing. I had to sit down at my desk to program my first Christmas that way.

I began to write, *Making memories with the ones you love* and *With us, you're always home for Christmas*, And stacked song after song that brought back memories of Mom Decking the Halls with Boughs of Holly. I completely, totally unraveled. As I tried to climb into the Christmassy heart of our listener, mine cracked like ice. I was alone. There would never be another *home for Christmas*. Even the girl screaming in my head was bawling her eyes out.

I sat in that cubby and cried so deeply and so silently, fearing the giant HUUUUHHH inhale you always do when you are weeping that hard. Oh, God, I thought, this office will *know* I'm nuts. I can't move my shoulders up and down. Don't let them see you. What if someone comes and tries to talk to me. I'm sunk. I'm a mess. I can't hide this. I can't do this. I can't write Christmas. I can't.

I staggered out of my cubby and into my boss's door. I shut it behind me and poured myself into a chair where I tried to speak but couldn't.

Mark's eyes went wide. "What IS it?"

"I can't do it," I whispered. "I can't."

"Yes, you can. You got this." He leaned back in his black leather chair and shook his Magic 8 ball. "Did you see the book? Your station's number one. Did you do three things to make your station better today?"

I nodded. "I did."

"The Magic Eight Ball says you can make it." He showed me the ball. "See, it says 'Yes. Definitely.' DEFINITELY Shannyn. The Ball doesn't lie."

I wanted so bad to laugh and buck up. Drink some water and head back to work, but I really was done. Empty. I had zero left. I barely smiled. "Mark. Really." I couldn't say much more.

"Does anything help?" he said, uncrossing his legs and leaning toward me on his desk.

"Gardening, but it's so cold." I sobbed too loud for this environment. I couldn't help it. "There's snow."

Tears heaved out of my chest like a waterfall. Poor Mark. He must have felt like he was caught in the estrogen ER. He got up and closed the heavy glass door.

"Then *garden,*" he said. "Who cares if it's cold? Go home right now and do something in your garden, OK?" I actually laughed a little. "Will you get out of here? You're freaking out the sales people."

I sprung Alex from daycare and booked it home, where I made Alex and me some cocoa with mini marshmallows. We cuddled up on the couch as she read her Richard Scarry and I my *Hamlet*. Hamlet, you say. Why, *yes*. Fancy, huh?

Hamlet is one of those plays I could read and read and always get something new and exciting from it. I'd read it hundreds of times. It was a security blanket for me, my Hamlet. It was proof that there are beautiful things in the world.

With Alex at my side on our little pink loveseat and Hamlet in one hand and a cup of cocoa to match hers in the other, I could say for certain that I enjoyed that moment. For a moment there, the scream was silent and all was well.

I flew through scene after delicious scene, picturing Ophelia and Hamlet in jeans and leather jackets, until I came to the part that always killed me: where Ophelia (you know, the one who's going nuts and drowns herself?) actually *goes* nuts over her father's death.

Now, there are all kinds of juicy layers to the story but in short, she flips because her dad died – and not just died but was accidentally murdered by her boyfriend, Hamlet, who basically turns on her and pulls the old "I never loved you" – the same basic trick as John. I was having a *girl, I feel you* moment when she bursts into the Queen's chambers and demands:

OPHELIA: Where is the beauteous majesty of Denmark? *(She's looking for Hamlet's mom, the queen)*

QUEEN GERTRUDE: How now, Ophelia! (*That means 'what's up, Ophelia?'*)

OPHELIA: (*Singing a timeless and haunting song*)

How should I your true love know

From another one?

By his cockle hat and staff,

And his sandal shoon. (OK, not timeless in a top 40 way, but still…)

QUEEN GERTRUDE: Alas, sweet lady, what imports this song? (Basically "what's up?")

OPHELIA: Say you? Nay, pray you, mark. (*Shhh! Listen*)

(Continuing to sing)

He is dead and gone, lady,

He is dead and gone;

At his head a grass-green turf,

At his heels a stone.

QUEEN GERTRUDE: Nay, but, Ophelia,— (*that's Shakespeake for "Oh, Ophelia honey, you're losing it.*)

OPHELIA: Pray you, mark.

(Continuing to continue . . .)

White his shroud as the mountain snow,—

Larded with sweet flowers

Which bewept to the grave did go

With true-love showers.

(she's talking about Daddy's tomb...in the snow.)(2)

This is what is commonly called *Ophelia's Mad Scene.* She rambles on in seemingly disjointed thoughts that always bring her back to lost love and a suddenly orphaned state. She's left with only her brother. This was my first time snuggling up with my Hamlet since the tornado, and Ophelia's grief blindsided me.

I remembered standing on the grounds of the house. I remembered the dirty floor and the people everywhere and the thought: You can crack up right now if you want. No one will blame you, Shannyn. Anyone would. You can go ahead and spend your whole life quiet in a white room, just rocking back and forth. Someone will take care of Alex. Someone will feed you.

But I chose not to. I chose to hold on for that little girl next to me reading and smelling like strawberry shampoo. I read on.

OPHELIA: I hope all will be well. We must be patient: but I cannot choose but weep, to think they should lay him in the cold ground. (I think we all get that point) My brother shall know of it! (and that one, too): and so I thank you for your good counsel. Come, my coach! Good night, ladies; good night, sweet ladies; good night, good night.

The tears started again, and I thought, "Good God! I am so sick of *crying*! The scream was on high in the background. But I kissed Alex on the head and remembering my promise to Mark I said, "It's nap time princess. You don't have to sleep, but you have to close your eyes and rest for a little bit. Mommy's gonna go play in the garden."

"OK, Mommy," she said.

I tell you, she was the best little girl in the world.

Once she was tucked in I grabbed my gardening gloves, a hand rake and shovel and headed to my garden. The chain link gate creaked slowly open, arthritic with the ice in its joints, and my rubber boots slushed through the crusty snowy yard. This is nuts, I thought. This is totally crazy. If someone sees me they will say for sure, "She's bought the farm."

But ...as Janice Joplin said, "Freedom's just another word for nothing left to lose" and so I knelt down amongst the herbs, the long-gone sage and thyme and the wilted chives, and brushed the ice and mud-caked leaves away from their roots.

"I've neglected you," I said. "I'm sorry. I will try to do better in the spring." I was talking out loud to plants. The step to talking to Mom and Dad wasn't a large one.

"Mom, Dad," I said, voice desperate, like a child lost in the mall or left behind at the circus. Gazing straight ahead into the midday snow, I squinted my eyes to see if they appeared. Blinded by the golden explosion of sunlight on the glassy drift, I didn't see them, but I still said out loud, "I miss you. I don't know what to do. I don't know how to live. I'm so lost."

I brushed the face of the soft sage brush with the back of my hand, and the plant talked back with a warm waft of oil. "And I'm so sick of crying." I said, lacing my fingers into the bright herbal braches. I squeezed it tight. "Sage is supposed to bring me peace."

I crushed the brown, frozen leaves between my fingers and inhaled deep as I could, filling every corner of my lungs with the smell of sage and snow and tears. "I don't know what to do. Are you there?

Where are you? I feel like I'm losing you and I don't know what to do. What if I forget you?"

Then I remembered Ophelia's line, "Here's rosemary, that's for remembrance. I pray you sirs, remember....Rosemary, for … remembrance."

"Rosemary helps memory," I said. I shook the rosemary bush by the plant's root and snow flew off like water from a just-bathed puppy dog.

I squatted down and rolled the weight back on my heels as the last of the snow and ice shot free. My eyes opened wide at the sun which shone in the crystal coldness. The rosemary was fresh, new, and perfect. Alive. It was anything but dormant. It was thriving as if this were a summer day.

I shoved my nose into the heart of the plant and inhaled.

"Don't forget, Shannyn. Don't forget. Who they were. That they were. That *we* were."

It was so cold; I feared my tears would freeze icicles on my lashes and cheeks. But through my sorrow, roots of faith were burrowing into the frozen spirit. A light deep inside my chest softened the shield around my heart. Something good, something God was happening.

And the edges of my lips, they remembered how to turn up. The muscles around my eyes gave way to the unfamiliar memory of a smile. Oh, Ophelia. I will remember.

"Exit," said the stage directions.

I ran inside for the scissors to clip some to bring in as proof that it truly *was* alive in the snowy cold of winter, as sure as summer rosemary, for remembrance. I somehow knew it was God, but I still had no idea what that would come to mean.

Mark gave me an *atta girl* nod when I returned to work the next day with a budvase of rosemary for my desk and a story of hope to pass along. He was probably grateful that I actually returned and wasn't at home cracking up, which at the time was a clear and present danger.

Mark…what a great boss, mostly because he trusted me and for that, I gave him my full allegiance. I don't think it's possible to under-estimate the power of knowing that someone has your back. That's one of the many reasons why losing my parents, even at age 29, was so devastating. Our parents are the only two people on the planet that we know have our back and always will. At least, they should. It was a scary feeling flying solo out there, especially when I knew nothing of our heavenly Father who never leaves or forsakes us. Mark filled that gap for me in a small way.

Still, my thinly cultivated peace cracked like a gingerbread house the day at work when Mark walked past my cubby and the smell of rosemary mixed with Mark's coffee and hazelnut cream. Something was wrong. I didn't even have to turn around to see it. I could feel it. I could hear it in the way he slammed his door.

Spinning my chair around I saw him through his glass wall. He was on the phone, and he was angry. He was also packing up his fa-vorite books, *The Cola Wars, The NBC Guide to Pronunciation*. Why was he packing his books up? He *used* those books every day.

"What's wrong?" I mouthed in slow motion. He just shook his head, "I'm fine," he mouthed back. But he was not. He was packing. He was downloading his phone list.

Mark emerged twenty minutes later with the news: the station was "Going in another direction" and he was let go.

All I could say was "What? Why?"

"For some excuse." he said. His Native American face was lined with stress and an instant burden of age.

"Mark, if you're gone, I'm gone," I said. "For real."

He shook his head. "No, don't do that, kid. This has nothing to do with you."

But at the time, it did. Mark was what kept me together. I could not conceive of the transition to a new boss. I honestly did not think I was strong enough. What other boss would say, "Go home and play in your garden," instead of "Get it together" when – and it *was* "when" not "if" – I crumbled at work? I was a train wreck. People couldn't help but slow down to get an eye full of the tornado girl flipping out while writing Christmas liners in her cubby.

My station was number one in the market. It was a good paying job. And I walked right out the door with Mark that day. Was that wise? No. Would I do it again? Probably. I knew I couldn't stand. Mark was my safety net, my bumper. He protected me. He covered me.

Alex's dad was picking her up at the on-site day care center that day and I told him the news.

His reaction? "You WHAT?"

"I said I quit today. They fired my boss and I can't do it without him and not only that but I don't owe you an explanation. You lost that right." I could feel the bitterness rising. I basically had no control over any of my emotions at that point, but I lowered my voice to mask my tone for Alex. "I'm only telling you because you will be picking up Alex at our house on Fridays now, not here."

"OK. OK, then. Fine."

His voice was tired and resigned. You created this mess, I thought! Sorry it's *hard* on you.

"Alex, come on," he said. "Give Mom a kiss goodbye. We've got a long trip."

With a "Mwah," and a squishy smooch and a smile and a wave, she was off with him.

I hated that part. The transition. The playing nice. The leaving. It was almost like having to relive his leaving again and again and to be honest I did not want to be civil. I wanted to tell him to lose my number and walk the other way if we should ever bump into each other. I only chose peace for Alex but the sight of John triggered my fight or flight response. Most days, I chose fight. That night, I chose flight. To a café, to work on my laptop and escape into the heart beat of music.

Yes, I said work. It only took me about fifteen minutes of thinking about living on my savings to realize that wasn't the smartest thing to do. I only quit in my mind.

My friend Sista Otis was playing Xhedos (a great music café) that night and she was always a slam dunk to lift my spirits. So I popped my laptop open and got down to it. I was scheduling music for Valentine's Day-the 107 Koolest Love Songs. It was a count day. I'd made it through Christmas as a Program Director, now it was time to make it through love day. Lame, but I knew I could do it.

I grabbed a great Sumatran coffee from the press pot and slid through the crowd of 20-somethings. It smelled like patchouli and coffee and sweat as the opening act began. The light and gangly nature boy with a leprechaun face was setting up and plugging in.

"Check. Check one two," he said as he strummed his acoustic with a smile.

What a nice guy, I thought. The people in his life must be so blessed to know him. I pulled out my pc and searched for the outlet in the nearly dark room.

"Hi, I'm Spider Joe," he said with a spark, "and this is a song about my dog."

I remembered that feeling you have when you're seven or eight years old and you know that boys are boys and girl are girls and you are different, but you don't care, you can just play-build a sandcastle all day and lose track of time without ever wondering if they *like* you. They like you. They're playing with you. I thought of sitting under a tree with him. It made me remember before it was a biggie if your friend was a boy.

He began to sing a wonderful celebration of his pooch...Buddy. "Me and my dog, my Buddy dog, we like to howl all night long. BAWOO!!!"

This guy's a riot, I thought, sipping my coffee and tapping away at my keyboard. He played a couple more crunchy granola songs followed by a couple tree hugger songs and then, with his set done, He made a b-line for my table.

"Hi, I'm Joseph," he said with a Richie Cunningham smile.

"Hi Joseph, I'm Shannyn," I said. "Nice to meet you. Nice set, man." I looked back to my work and began to type again.

"Do you like art?"

"Me? Art? No I can't stand it. I wish people would quit trying to express themselves." I rolled my eyes, "Of course I like art."

"Do you like Van Gogh? The Van Gogh exhibit is at the Detroit Institute of Arts!"

I kept my face fixed on my screen. This guy was a real sweetie, but I was not interested in dating anyone, ever again, period and I was pretty sure that's what he was getting at.

"Do you have a phone number, an email address, anything?" he pressed me.

"No, I don't have those things." I shrugged. "I'm a Luddite."

"Really?" His blue eyes widened.

"No, not really. I have both those things. Do you?"

"Yes. Yeah, sure hang on," he said.

He fumbled for paper and pen at the register, and he scratched down his info and passed it to me just as Sista Otis struck her first chord and the joint got nice and loud.

"It's too loud to talk," I shouted.

Joe nodded agreement. "A pleasure making your acquaintance," he shouted back with a gleam.

I nodded and tipped my head good-bye, while holding the paper with his number. Should I keep it? I thought. Why not? Maybe some-day I would need someone to write a song for my cat.

CHAPTER 5

WHY CAN'T WE BE FRIENDS?

Lord, thank you for the times you bring sweet memories to mind, like when Mom would say, "Patience is a virtue," and we would laugh and recite the entire Irish proverb: "Patience is a virtue. Possess it if you can. Seldom found in women and never found in men."

"So, how's your week been?" my therapist Laura said, crossing her legs. Her khakis were perfectly creased. She grabbed my ever thickening manila file out of her briefcase.

"Well…it's been good, except, they fired Mark and I feel like I'm falling off a cliff."

"Really," she said "Um, would you like to expand on that at all?"

"OK."

I began to fidget with my nails and repositioned my legs one way, then the other. I was trying to put it together without walking away with a brand new extra nutty diagnosis, but finally I elected to throw caution to the wind and tell it, as they say, like it is.

I planted my feet and leaned forward in my wingback chair. "Sure. They fired Mark. And I love Mark. Mark has my back. Mark's the one

I trust. He's stood up for me a million times." I was rocking back and forth in my chair. "I don't know, Laura. I really hate the idea of doing this job without him."

"Hum...what do you "hate" about that idea?" She placed her air quotes.

"I hate not having a safety net."

"Mark's your safety net?"

"Kinda..."

"He's your boss? Mark?"

I nodded.

"So Mark's your safety net and he got fired. Hum...Do you know WHY he got fired?"

"I don't. He didn't say. No one's talking."

"I mean...was it dramatic," she said. "Was it civil? I mean, can you share a little about how that played out?" She rubbed her hands expectantly.

"Well, Mark was let go after the end of the work day. You know how we always stay late. It was like that...last Friday. It's like 6:30. I'm working. Alex's playing on her Leap Pad in her little cubby of my desk. So Mark's in my big boss's office...talking. Then Mark walks out, closes his office door and gets on the phone then packs up his stuff and leaves. He didn't say what happened." I reached for my hand cream.

"Did you see this coming at all?"

"Not at all." I took a big inhale of the cranberry lotion. "I asked Ron, my big boss, if everything was OK with Mark and he just said, 'Well, kiddo, Mark won't be with us any more' and patted me on the back on his way out the door."

"Wow. How did that make you feel?"

"I don't know, confused? Mad? Scared? Plus the 'kiddo' thing is never my fave."

"You really like Mark, don't you?" She leaned into me over her crossed legs.

"I do. I really do. I like Mark." I suddenly felt like there might be a hidden camera, like I was being observed, which…I was.

"What do you like about him?"

"Well, he's smart. He's kind. He's got a great voice. He likes Indian food. He took a risk on me. He loves music. He lives on a sail boat. He's a hot Native American. Seriously, girl. Mom and Dad are the ones who wanted me to marry an Irish Catholic. I wanted to grow up and marry an Indian Chief and live in a teepee, but a sailboat would do. He loves kids. It's his one regret in life, that he's never been a father. Want me to go on? He loves God."

"Well…it sounds as if you *really* like Mark. Why didn't you do anything about this, then?" Her eyes locked on mine as she scribbled notes on her yellow pad.

"I do. I do really like Mark. But there is absolutely nothing there." I grabbed my coffee off the table, "He was my boss so there was nothing. I wish." I shrugged, "But that's just sad and lame me. I don't *really* wish. I just like to *wish* I wished." I grabbed my Chapstick, anything to keep my hands busy. "You know me. I'm done." I fumbled to get the top off, "Plus, he likes girls with bodies that look way different than mine." I applied the cherry balm, the same kind I'd used since I was 7, "He likes red lipstick, tight clothes. It's kind of embarrassing. But, he's a rocker and I'm just a geeky heartbroken single mom." I put the stick away with finality.

"Things at work OK so far this week?"

"Yep." I'd already decided not to tell her I quit and then changed my mind. I came across crazy enough as it was.

"So, anything else happen?" Laura drummed the desk with her pencil. "As if that weren't enough, right?"

"Well, I did meet a nice man." I rolled my eyes and smiled.

"Really?" Laura perked up more than usual, even for her. "Tell me more about this nice man."

"His name is Joseph and he's a musician. He was opening for my friend Otis when I went to hear her play on Friday."

"So what makes him nice?"

"He just seemed really bright. Friendly." I peeked at my phone to check the time. Suddenly we were at a crawl, "He was just really himself, ya know. I just liked him. He looked like he goes camping. He looked like he'd be comfortable in the woods. I like that. I miss the woods, here in Detroit."

She bobbed her crossed leg up and down. "Hum…so did you talk? I'm assuming you talked."

"Yep. We talked. He came over to my table while I was working and tried to chat it up."

"Tried?" She smiled. "Were you mean to him? You weren't mean to him, were you?"

"Yeah," I said with a cast-off shrug. "I pretty much shut him down."

"What do you mean by shut him down? Was he flirting? I mean… coming on schmoozy?"

"Well, I guess, not schmoozy…not really flirty, he wasn't Rico Suave' but I think he *was* asking me out."

"Can you tell me what happened?"

I told her about, "I hate art and wish people would quit trying to express themselves and no I'm a Luddite," and her eyes popped. "YOU DIDN'T! Are you serious?"

Laura had been my therapist for so long, it sometimes felt like friendship. I wasn't sure that was good.

"Yes," I said. "But he gave me his info in case I ever want to chat."

"Did you keep the number?"

"Yep. It's in my planner." I Vanna-Whited around my black leather Day-Timer, the one I'd set up because Laura had been suggesting I organize my schedule.

She gave me a golf clap. "Why were you so mean to him? Do you see that could be perceived as mean, perhaps, by someone who was a little sensitive?"

"It was fine. He knew I was joking. I don't know. I just, I well…I'm never, never interested in dating again." I shoved the binder into my messenger bag. "I'm fine. I have no room in my life for a relationship." I snapped the bag shut. "Not a boyfriend. I have enough on my plate just worrying about me and Alex, let alone some random guy." Just the thought of romantic involvement shortened my breath and triggered my gag reflex.

"OK…I understand, but do you have room for a new *friend?*"

"Sure. I guess."

"And would it be OK if that friend were a boy? I mean…..you can still have boy *friends,* right?"

I'd never quiet thought of it like that. I took another slow inhale. "I suppose that would be OK, yes."

"OK, just checking." Laura smiled, once again crossing her legs.

"No. It's OK. I have tons of guy friends. Brett, Michael, Julian, Phil, Jason…tons. I like guys better than girls."

"Uh-huh." She rolled her eyes back in her head. Her glare clearly read: "I didn't just meet you."

"I'm not a man hater," I said.

But I was defending a falsehood, because in truth, I didn't love men all that much. Even my best guy friends were hound dogs behind closed doors. Men were on shaky ground with me. I was very fond of the ultimate imaginary dream man who moves big stuff and tells me I'm pretty all while rockin' the laundry and bonding with woodland creatures and babies. But I did not entertain the idea that said man actually existed. I didn't hate men. It was more like I feared them and I was pretty set on making sure they feared me too.

But Laura was right, there was no good reason to fear or hate that nice guy named Joseph and he did seem to know where the woods were hidden around Detroit.

I decided to give him a call.

His voice sounded tentative when he answered. And young—he sounded young. Teenaged.

"Hi. Is this Joseph?" I said . . . instead of hanging up, which was what I wanted to do.

"Yes...this is Joseph."

"Hi, Joseph. This is Shannyn. I met you the other night at Xhedo's?" I heaped an extra helping of casual into my voice.

"Oh, HI!" Joseph's voice lit up like a Christmas tree. "How's it going? You called me! Cool! I didn't think you would."

"Well, you seem like a nice guy and I like nice people so..."

"Well . . . so . . . how's it going?"

I scooped some hazelnut coffee into the French press coffee pot. *How's it going? That's all ya got?* I thought.

"It's good. It's really good," I said. But I was thinking this kind of lame conversation was the reason I didn't bother making new friends. If I was talking to an actual friend, we'd already be onto "how was your day and do you want to go get Thai food?" but instead we were starting at the very beginning.

"So tell me about yourself," Joseph said. He sounded like a 12 year old hiding behind the school with a girl at recess.

I didn't really *want* to tell him about myself because I was a corrupted wasteland of wrecked marriage and dead parents and no one, I thought, wanted to be mixed up with someone like that. But it was what it is was and so, as I did with Laura, I cut to the chase.

I gave my elevator pitch.

"I'm a single mom of a beautiful five year old daughter. I work full time. My hobby is yoga and meditation. I love music. I love Shakespeare. I love chocolate and gardening and long walks. My parents were killed not too long ago and so at the moment I'm a little bit sad. That is a giant understatement. I'm a little broke. Sometimes I drop stuff and that may always be so. I have great friends and a strong right hook."

Joe gave a nervous chuckle and to my surprise did not hang up. "Well, I don't have a girlfriend or anything…" he said his voice a little shaky, "Do you ever wanna hook up?"

"Do I want to hook up?" I repeated his question slowly back at him, "I don't think I hook up." I put on my best Scarlet O'Hara, "I'm not a hook up kind of girl, Joseph Caldwell."

He actually stammered. "No, no, not *hook up*! Yeesh! I need to be careful with my words! I mean like, hang out? Get to know each other, or whatever?"

Joseph sounded as awkward as I did but he had no excuse. He was out there in the dating world in full swing, from what my sources told me. But this was not a date we were talking about. It was getting to know a new friend.

"Sure. Yeah. That would be nice," I said. "I'd like to get to know you, Joseph Caldwell."

"I'd like to get to know you, too, Shannyn Cook. Want to have lunch on Saturday? Thai? Do you like Thai?"

Finally we were getting somewhere! Talk to me, Thai food lover.

"I love Thai. Thai would be great some time, but I was thinking you sing a lot of songs about the woods and lakes." I took a big sip of coffee.

"Yeah, yep."

"And ya know, I'm from the U.P." I grabbed the chocolate milk from the fridge and poured a big glob in my cup. Mmm, hazelnut mocha. *See there's good stuff in this world*, I thought, "Yeah. Have you been to the U.P.? It's pretty much all woods up there."

I was talking about Michigan's Upper Peninsula—mostly woods and moose and bars and churches. If you ever go there, eat a pasty. You will thank me.

"Sure. Yeah," he said. He said that a lot. "You're from the U.P.? Awesome. I love the U.P."

"I've been here in Detroit for like five years now and I can't seem to find any woods to go hike in." I hoped I'd finally found a Detroiter who'd understand the need for a walk in the woods. "I don't mean a park with paths, I mean woods. Where it's quiet and you don't see other people. Are there any woods around here?"

"Oh sure, yeah. I mean you have to drive for a while, but yeah. There's lots of woods. Paint Creek is nice. You ever been to Paint Creek?"

"Nope. Never heard of it." I smelled the yummy mug and pondered what woods called "Paint Creek" might be like.

"You've never heard of Paint Creek?" Joseph gave new voice to the word 'flabbergasted.' "Well, that's where you want to go. You want to go to Paint Creek with me, Shannyn Cook?"

"Well, how 'bout this." I warmed my cup up and stirred it while I thought about what I wanted to do, rather than just agreeing to go. I decided to switch the plan a bit as the scene of my body being dragged out of the woods on the evening news flashed through my mind. "Why don't we meet for breakfast and then if we feel like it, we can go check it out," I said.

I would check out with friends how cool Paint Creek was to them or if it was a freaky meet-up park and then screen Joseph over breakfast to see how much I wanted to go to the woods with him.

"OK. Good idea," he said. "We'll fuel up for our hike. Do you know where Alex's is in Berkley? Wanna meet there?"

"Sure," I said, and thought how crazy it was that he was suggesting our first meeting be at a restaurant that bore the same name as my little girl. And how strange to meet two handsome Josephs in a year!

"8:30. I'll see you there."

I realized I *was* excited about the prospect, but I was also determined to not let it side-track me from dealing with my grief. I needed to stay focused on healing so I could really, fully heal. I didn't want a distraction. I wanted a friend.

I knew the minute that I slid into the sticky vinyl booth that I was in big trouble. Joseph was beautiful in his blue long johns shirt and jeans. He was the type that makes most girls melt. He could get paid to dance for screaming housewives at casinos. Thankfully, he was not my type. He was ripped. I liked nerds. He was wearing a baby-blue yarn necklace, holding a little girl charm around his neck, the kind moms wear on golden chains. He was all buff *and* loved the little children. It was romance novel crazy.

I gestured to it. "Who's that little girl necklace for?"

His eyes opened even wider. "Oh this?" He smiled and pulled it up to his lips for a kiss. "This is for my niece, Elizabeth. She is so beautiful. All my nieces are beautiful."

How cute is this guy? I thought. Or is he a creeper? We shall see.

"How many nieces do you have?" I said.

"Three nieces and a nephew," he smiled, pulling back his shoulders, "my brothers are family men." He poured one cream and half a sugar into the brown glazed mug. "Mostly. The youngest. Well...." He tucked the remaining sugar under his napkin. "Do you know what you want? Are you ready to order?"

I nodded. "So how many siblings do you have?"

"Me and three brothers. All boys." He waved the server over. "Mom had her hands full."

"Wow." I sighed thinking, great...so he knows zero about women. Goody. I can only imagine trying to polish my fingernails in a house with this charmer. Eew! It smells.

"You? Siblings?" he asks.

"Yes," I said as the server approached, pen ready. "A brother. Ryan and he's my very best buddy in the universe."

"Hi. Y'all ready?" The mousy haired waitress smiled from under her red-striped bandana.

Joe gestured to me. I noticed his hands were uber-strong. Workman's hands. Worn. Cut and calloused in juxtaposition to his gentle smile and tender eyes. Too bad I didn't meet this guy before I blew my life up. Too bad I couldn't think of him romantically. But we can be buds, I told myself. I can tell him which women are not evil and make sure he doesn't date bimbos. Oh no, I though. I hope he doesn't date bimbos. I'm not sure we can be friends if he does. I snap back to reality and order.

"I'll have three egg whites, wheat toast dry and sliced tomatoes, please." I glanced at Joseph. "Yeah. I'm that girl."

"Oh, honey, you'd be surprised the things people ask for," the waitress said. "That's nothing. How 'bout you, Joe?"

"I'll have the special, over medium, wheat toast, sausage links, pancakes and more coffee, please."

"Very good and I'll be right back with that coffee."

I smiled at him when she was gone. "Joe, huh?"

"Oh, yeah. I come here a lot. Some people call me Joe, but I prefer Joseph."

"OK, Joseph it is."

We downloaded our basic information over bad coffee.

Joseph: 35. Never married. Self- employed construction worker, tree-trimmer, kid-loving son of an alcoholic. Music-playing, recycling nature-head with a dog named Buddy who had his own theme song. I liked him.

Shannyn: Single mother, divorced. Heart-broken radio baby with a house and a degree and great friends. Spiritual, rude, kickboxing yoga mama which a heart of gold and an axe to grind.

With bellies full of eggs and heads full of ideas, we stacked our empty plates at the end of the table. "Whelp, You ready? Ya got good shoes on? It's a little rough." He bent his neck to check my footwear. "I mean, there's a path, but..."

"I'm good. Let's go." I hiked my bag across my chest and zipped up my hoodie.

"Wanna ride together?" he asked with a shrug.

"Naw," I said. "I'll drive separately just in case. I've got a new d.j. starting at the station today and I want to be able to zip out there fast if he freaks out."

That was partly true. I did want to be able to get away fast if my jock freaked out. Or I freaked out. Or Joseph freaked out.

"I'll follow you, OK?" I said.

"Yeah, for sure." He sounded disappointed. "I'm in a red Ford pick- up. I'll pull up. This is you, right?" He pointed to my green CR-V. "I saw you pull in."

"Yep, that's me," I said. I was surprised he was on the lookout for me. Maybe good, maybe weird.

It was, as Daddy used to say, "A hop, skip and a jump" to the Paint Creek Forest. What a relief it was to step out of my car and hear the crunch of dry leaves under my feet. It smelled like birch and pine and dirt . . . a welcome change from the stench of factories and freeways in the city. I took a deep inhale to every corner of my lungs and felt a natural smile cross my lips. It was the first spontaneous smile I could remember since the tornado. Cool, I thought, my smile still works!

Joseph joined me in the parking lot with his own smiling eyes, "Glad you could keep up," he said, his wink joking with me, "You drive like a grandma."

I smiled back. Yep, the smile...works!

"Well," He shrugged, "Let's go check it out."

It suddenly felt good *not* being on a date with Joseph. I didn't give a singular thought of how my hair was holding up, or if my lipstick was gone, or if my eyes were going all Tammy Faye. I didn't worry about how skinny I looked in my cords. This was a friend who knew where the woods were and who was glad to show me around.

"Well," Joe was digging in his coat pockets—for gloves, I figured out, "There's a river, with a path, ya know. We could walk along there. It's cold. You got gloves?"

"Sounds great and yes."

I could feel my shoulders start to unwind from around my ears as I took big deep breaths of the fresh and crispy winter air. We trudged along the muddy path by the river where a beaver had definitely been getting busy. "I love how those deep chop marks look. They're so cute. I wonder if we'll see one."

"Maybe," Joe picked up a pinch of the wood chippings left behind by the busy beast"It's amazing the way they do that, right?" he said chomping the air with his two front teeth. "That's some strong teeth right there."

"Right? Can you imagine? And the way they swim? Cool tails." My breath was struggling a little. Joseph was trucking. He wasn't kidding "good shoes."

"How you doing?" he asked, looking over his shoulder to check.

"I'm good," I said, and it was true. I was surprisingly good. "My feet are getting wet though. I wish I had better socks. Smartwool socks! Have you ever tried Smartwool socks?"

"Yeah, yeah I love Smartwool socks. They're the bomb."

"They have those built in arch supports!"

"They hug your feet." Joe's eyes were huge.

"I love them. I wish I had them on right now. I wish I had on Smartwool socks and these boots that my friend Dolly makes. She's a boot maker with the Renaissance Festival."

Joe stopped his stride on the path. "I know your friend Dolly."

I stopped too. "You do?"

"Yes. Sure. I delivered your note!" and his Irish eyes smiled even more. He had the stars…the ones from the youth group and Aunt Jane.

As I stood there in the crunchy winter air the face of Joseph, my sweet new dark-haired, blue-eyed nature-boy, friend from the coffee shop snapped . . . superimposed on the face of that handsome, *hot* long- haired, green-eyed Joseph I met . . .when I was at Delia's for breakfast. The one who said he believed in fairies.

"WHAT?" I waited to see if my scream would echo. "Why didn't you TELL me?"

Smiling just like a kid caught being naughty, Joseph said, "Because, if I told you and you didn't remember, I would look like an idiot for remembering. And if I told you and you *did* remember I'd look like an idiot for bringing it up."

I knew right then and there that I was in great big giant heaps of trouble. I had no idea why I didn't recognize him. I mean, at Delia's it was the end of summer, his skin was dark, his hair long and bleached out from working in the sun. Now, he was pale. His hair was cut short. The highlights were gone. His eyes turned from blue to green and back.

I'd had no idea at all and it was a good thing. If I *had* known it was him, I would have been too intimidated to hang out. After all, you can't un-hot a guy. Once the heat is turned on there's nothing you can do. Sure, it can be like chili. You put in too many peppers and you're afraid people won't be able to take the heat, that your kids will cry and spit it out, and the only option, is . . . you add sugar. Sugar cuts the heat. It makes it bearable.

But with men, it's the opposite. Oh sure, sugar cuts the heat, but it makes it unbearable. I for one knew I could not think straight around that guy from the restaurant, but *this* guy . . . he was softer, almost geeky. I liked him and I decided I could get past his potential gorgeousness and still be his friend.

It was a "don't hate me because I'm beautiful" moment.

Superman was hidden in Clark Kent and that worked out just fine, because at the moment I wasn't the least bit interested in being rescued. I only wanted a hike in the woods. A hike in the woods and . . .

"Thai food?" Joe said. "It's cold. It'll warm us up. There's a good place around the corner if you're ready to hoof it back."

"Yes."

What transpired was the world's longest first, not-a-date which ended with a tiny kiss that Joseph placed delicately in the smile lines of my right cheek.

It was lovely and it would be so much fun to tell you all the stories of sharing the news with my Jewish friends, the ones who love me and held me up and sat Shiva with me. I'd *love* to tell you all about the way they scrutinized, evaluated, dissected and eventually approved of and rejoiced in Joseph David Caldwell, suggesting he surely was of the 12 tribes of Israel and just *thought* he was Irish.

It would be a blast to tell you about our proposal . . . how he bought both me *and* Alexandra diamond rings and got on his knees to us at a wonderful Italian restaurant.

I'd love to and maybe someday I will, either in person over spaghetti ourselves one day.

This story, though, isn't meant to be a story about how I had been heartbroken by divorce and a tornado and then met a really great guy and fell in love and lived happily ever after. It's not a story about how my grief was healed because Joseph loved me. It's a story about how my grief was healed because Jesus loved me.

But yes! I did fall in love with and get married to Joseph on a steamy Michigan day in June. His dad (named Two Birds; kinda close to an Indian name, right?) had been ordained on the Internet with the Universal Life Church because no pastor or minister would agree to marry us and we didn't want to go to a judge. So Two Birds did the deed and married us under a maypole in the woods, with a drum circle of children and everything.

It was a beautiful wedding and everyone said so, and the whole thing cost only $300-food and everything . . . including the rings!

Less than two years later we had a little boy and named him Liam as an Irish tip of the hat to my daddy, Leon. With our boy and girl and white-fenced suburban house, you would think that we could sit back, relax and enjoy the good life.

What we both commenced to do instead was to grow to hate our lives and each other. The Bible says the Lord draws near to the broken hearted. I'd seen it in the wreckage of the tornado. Now I was seeing it prove true again, as my dreamy, gentle friend Joseph began to turn on me. I didn't know what was happening. I *knew* I was a disaster myself, but I never expected *him* to become my accuser. My house was caught in the eye of a whole new storm. But the one who calms the storms...well, He had His eye on me...on us. His name is Jesus and he was about to walk into the middle of our awful, beautiful mess and make it a healing season.

CHAPTER 6

WELCOME TO THE PARTY

Father, I know that you are the God of salvation. You led the people of
Israel from bondage and slavery to hope and freedom.
I am trusting you to do the same with me.

Joe turned out to be a yeller. Snapping my head off. Wearing his
Marine face. Throwing dishes, lamps, chairs.

And me? I cried nearly all the time. Three years into our marriage and I still walked on egg shells and cried daily.

I still dropped plates. My nerves were shot. Our baby never slept
and therefore neither did I.

I was exhausted. I was hopeless. I had done my best to follow
the yellow brick road laid out before me and I had gotten me, my
daughter and now a baby boy into a horrible, terrible mess. I'd always
wanted to program my own radio station, but the weight of the pressure and work and home and the new baby, I couldn't handle that
kind of responsibility. So I was working only part time as a fill-in disc
jockey for a cluster of three stations and helping the next in line at
Starbucks thirty hours a week. Bill collectors were calling non-stop.

What money I got from the insurance on Mom and Dad's house was nearly gone as the stock market plunged. It was getting to the point that I didn't even care.

Alex was growing so fast, and she was learning to ride a wave of a still-broken mother, a sometimes Jekyll and Hyde stepdad, a new baby brother and random broken dishes. It was ugly and *that* is what it looked like when I was trying my *best*. I was running to yoga every chance I could get, just to get out of the house and have someone talk to me in a gentle, kind voice and say, "Good. Soften. Breathe."

I was fried.

It was the weekend of the big Midwestern Blackout that my light started to turn on. I'd received an invitation to a party, a retirement party for some people I didn't know and didn't recognize. I had no idea who the adorable family of three on the front of the invite was and for my life couldn't figure how I knew them, *if* I knew them, and how in the wide world they had our address.

It made me nervous, as I was on the air at a local Detroit station and didn't love the idea of having my home address circulating.

Plus, the people on the invite were *young*. They looked 20-something. Who were they? Looking further, I realized that the party's address was on my block, so now I had to know how this was all fitting together. I strapped baby Liam into my Baby Bjorn and took a walk in the neighborhood to find the house where the party was to be held and ask how they knew us.

As it turned out, the party was, not surprisingly, being held at the house on the block that I called *The Party House*. Two young blondes had moved in about a year prior and since their arrival, I'd watched them sitting on the porch drinking and laughing by candlelight. And as my belly grew with the baby and my hips spread wider and wider still, I came to resent the young newcomers and their single-girl freedom.

Great, I'd think. As I'm getting huge, and my husband's complaining he can't even pass me in a room, *these girls* move in? Fabulous! More eye candy for Joseph and more comparisons for me. This just stinks.

But it was the address on the invite and so I trudged up the cement stairs and onto the party porch for the first time. After I knocked I saw one of the two, the blonder of the pair, coming to answer with a friendly smile. Her bright white teeth and blue eyes shone through the lead glass panes of the door. She had the twinkle of the youth group kids, too.

"Hi," she said like a kindergarten teacher.

"Hi. I'm Shannyn and this is Liam. We live across the street in that house with the vegetable garden." I felt like an old slouch next to this perky, white toothed goddess. I could never compete with that! But her unassuming demeanor surprised me and lowered my guard.

"Hi, sure, yes." She flashed a serene smile. "I'm Becky. The other girl who lives here is Rebecca. We're Becky and Rebecca."

"OK," I say. And I think, *How cute.*

And then my insecurity welled up as I noticed I had nasty dried breast milk all over my t-shirt. I'd looked so cute earlier that morning and there stood Becky, smelling like a Tide commercial. I thought: I'm sunk.

But I muddled on anyway. "So, I got an invite to a party here tonight, a retirement party, and I'm wondering who sent it and how you guys knew my name and address since we've never met."

"Hmm." She paused. "I don't know. I honestly don't." She paused again. "But I think you should come to the party. Do you think you can come?"

"Well, I'll have to check with my husband," I said, using my get-out-of-the-party-free card while establishing ownership of my man. "Nice to meet you, though."

"Yeah, nice to meet you! And you too, Liam." She reached out the perfect nails and pinched his tiny cheek.

I talked it over with Joseph, intentionally maintaining eye contact to make sure he couldn't sense my inferiority complex. He agreed, we should meet the neighbors.

"We'll tell 'em to keep it down," he joked. "We were the old people across the street to those girls."

That night was wild. There was a giant classic car event – in fact, the world's largest single day car event, the Woodward Dream Cruise – making its way down the end of the block. Millions of people and classic cars from all eras were flexing their muscles. People were always concerned there would be rioting when darkness fell on the crowd. Ah, the intersection of muscle cars, summer heat and too much Budweiser was best avoided.

Joseph and I decided to ditch the chaos of the cruise and instead go see what was up with these new neighbors who laughed under candlelight across the street. I put on a pretty tank top and flowery green skirt and felt fresh enough to face the young blondes. My make-up looked great. At least it was on for once. I was bronzed and glossed and I did *not* smell like rotten milk.

When we got there the party was on. It was packed. People were sampling their home brewed beer in the dining room. There was a group playing an imagination game called Murder in the back yard. A guitar was being strummed for a small group gathered on the candlelit porch. There was food everywhere. Great cheese and homemade crackers on every table. Fresh bread and chive butter with a kettle of soup in the kitchen. It was so simple and so extravagant.

I thought, one day these girls will have jobs and kids and then I'd like to see them try to make their own darned crackers.

The couple for whom the retirement party was being thrown was there, too, of course: Jim and Meg and their baby boy, Eli. Another couple was there with kids as well. This homebrew couple, Nate and Amy Kimball, had an itty bitty baby and a toddler.

I noticed two amazing things as the party went on. One: no one was getting drunk but everyone was having fun anyway. Two: the family units seemed to actually work. The husbands were kind to their wives and the wives had this strange honor or reverence for their husbands that reminded me of mail-order-brides, but with a *choice* to obey.

And speaking of obey . . . the kids, the toddlers, they obeyed, too. It was downright wild. It was crazy. It was weird. I'd never seen anything like it in all my days and I kind of wanted to know what the heck it was all about.

"OK, baby," beanpole Amy said to her two-year-old. "Mom and Dad are going to stay up and play with their friends a little longer, but it's time for *you* to get to bed. Miss Rebecca has your bed all set up with your favorite blanket and book. It's time to go and lay down now. Mom will be right in to tuck you, OK?"

And the kid... did it!

What?

For real?

How in the world did you do that? I thought. I want some of whatever that is, *now*.

"You look familiar," Meg said to me as we sat side by side on the steps on the front porch.

"I do?"

"Yes. I swear we've met before. Were you at the Pampered Chef party last fall?"

"Yes! Right!" I agreed, remembering the darling girl who was as pregnant as me at the time. "We exchanged phone numbers there."

"Yeah, we had just moved here from Chicago."

"And your hubby was working at Starbucks," I said.

"Right. Yes. This is his retirement party FROM Starbucks." She smiled from diamond studded ear to diamond studded ear, her nose crinkled up.

"Really?" I said. "Cool! I'm still working there. Maybe one day I'll be out, too. A girl can dream. What's he doing instead?"

"Well, it's actually what he's been doing all along. Starbucks was supplemental and for insurance, you know. But we moved here so Jim could be a pastor of a church."

"For real?" I felt my eyes popping from my head. "A pastor? You're a pastor's wife? Dude!"

Meg laughed. "You crack me up. Yes, for real. The church is doing well enough that he's been released to full time ministry. We *so* have to get together. Do you still have my number?"

I had to confess I didn't. "Do you still have mine?"

"No," she said, and we both had a good laugh.

And so we traded again and little did I know that a giant seed was officially planted.

"So, this is a church?" I said, in amazement.

"Yep. Jim's the pastor." Meg's voice bounced along with the baby on her hip and she jerked her head toward a very tall guy standing in the nearby driveway.

Jim tossed his long blonde hair out of his face with a smile and waved. I waved back as Meg continued. "And Rebecca's our women's minister. Have you met Rebecca yet? It's her house."

"Yep. We met out back. Her homemade bread's amazing."

I was trying to hide my combination of jealousy and lack of church lady skill. Please *God*, I thought, please don't have them start speaking church language. I don't speak it at all. I already feel weird enough being over here.

But I liked them. I could tell Joe liked them. They were cool. Little pockets of laughter bubbled up in the back and side yards as small groups shared candlelight under a summer starry sky.

"And this guy with the guitar is our worship leader, Nate." Jim made a sweeping motion with his long arm toward a bald headed, full bearded guy. "Nate's the one who provided the homebrew. Good stuff man," he said with a pat on Nate's back. "Did you guys want one? It's in the kitchen."

"Aw, no thanks, man. We're good. We're going soon." Joe put his arm around me and gave me a squeeze.

I was still hung up on 'worship leader.' "I have no idea what that is?" I said to Jim.

"He plays the music."

"You call the music worship?" It was like when a Southerner orders a Coke and what they want is a 7UP. The word didn't seem to match what it was.

"Yes…generally we do. Don't you think, Babe?" he asked Meg. She nodded.

"Wow, interesting." Strange, I thought, taking the entire meaning of the word "worship" and stealing it away only for music. Hmm.

"We call everything worship," I said. "Working in my garden. Paying my bills, everything."

Joe burst into a belly laugh. "Yeah … she worships while paying the bills. Is *that* what that's called? Worship? I worship when the Lions lose, then."

"But really," I said. "Cleaning, eating, sleeping, and taking a walk. It's all worship to us."

"Oh, are you guys Christians?" Meg sounded a bit surprised.

"Nope. We're some of the 'it's all one' people." I smiled at Joseph and peeked into Liam's baby carrier to make sure he was still safe and sound. He was out like a light.

"Yeah," Joe said, "we don't get hung up on us and them. We love God. We love people. We think God loves people, too." He set his shoulders back and took his Marine Corp stance.

"I'd love to talk to you more about that some time." Suddenly, Meg was squinting at me like I was a puzzle, or maybe a science project. I knew that at some point soon, she was going to try to save me and share the good news and I'd heard it *so* many times. I'd just let her bounce it off me. Say, "thank you for thinking of me" and keep on rolling in our budding friendship.

"Sure thing," I said. "Sounds great."

Rebecca stepped onto the porch from inside the chatty front room. She threw her sturdy arms all the way around me and squeezed. "I'm so glad you guys came."

"Us, too," Joseph said, and it was true. We'd had deepish and friendly conversations all night long and no one had flirted with either of us. Loved it. "Thanks for inviting us."

"Did you guys ever figure out how you got the invite?" Meg said.

"No idea. But we're glad we did." Joe reached for a blanket out of the diaper bag and tented sleeping Liam in his car seat. Meg checked on little Eli, sleeping in his seat next to Liam on the grass. "It's nice to meet you folks."

It really was nice to meet them. The women could have a conversation with my husband without hitting on him. I could talk to the guys without any weird vibes. They played board games. They had fun, real fun, clean fun. I'd never seen that in my adult life.

"We just thought this was a party house," I said. "And we approve of that, of course."

"A party house?" Rebecca responded with her huge voice, her grey eyes were even larger, "Why?"

"Well, look!" Joe said.

"Sure," I said, lacing my fingers in Joe's. "You guys have parties all the time. Ah, youth!"

"We do? When?"

"Like every week," I said. "Sometimes twice a week, but I notice always on Wednesdays. I call it your "Over the hump" party."

"Oh wow! Really?" Rebecca looked sharply at Meg, Meg shot an alarmed glace at Jim. Jim's face belonged on someone creeping in past curfew on creaky hardwoods. Jim tossed his hands up in surrender, "We have a bible study on Wednesdays. Maybe that's it. Should we keep it down?"

"No!" Joe said.

I gave my head a did-I-hear-you-right shake. "For real? That party is a Bible study?"

I'd never been to a Bible study or even seen one, but I can promise you that is not what I thought they would be like . . . young hipsters singing wildly under the moonlight, and chowing on goat cheese and blueberries. Saying words like "Dude" and "For real, man." And "Can I hold your baby?" Even my own family members never asked to hold the baby and give my arms a break! In my mind, a Bible study was a black and solemn event and they . . . were neon.

"Well," Meg said as she snapped the buckles on Eli's car seat, "we have to roll. Eli needs to get to bed."

Jim agreed with a nod as he tossed the diaper bag over his shoulder. "Thanks so much, Reba," he said giving Rebecca a brotherly embrace.

"You can tuck him in upstairs if you want to stay. I have a pack-n-play set up."

"Naw, that's OK." Meg laid a kiss on Rebecca's cheek. "We have to keep him in his routine. Thanks so much. I love you, my friend."

Routine, I thought. KEEP him in his routine? What kind of magic do these people have?

"Shannyn, Joseph," Jim said with a firm handshake to each of us, first Joe, then me. "It was great to meet you. I hope we run into each other again."

"Oh, we will," Meg said with a wink in my direction. "We will not miss our chance this time. I'll call you early in the week. I'm so stoked that we hooked up again, Shannyn. Jim...we have a story, Shannyn and I do. I'll tell you in the car."

And with that, the young pastor and his family loaded into the car and were out. So *that's* what a healthy family looks like, I thought. Cool.

Joe and I said our thank you and good-byes and headed home ourselves.

"Cool people, huh?" I said under my breath as we crossed the street.

"Yeah. Cool people." Joe said. He sounded as surprised as me.

I didn't get my hopes up about what a friendship might look like for Meg and me, but I did think in a perfect world, Meg really *would* call and we would hang out. I also knew the world…well, it wasn't perfect.

It was Monday when Meg called. I grabbed the phone with soapy hands as I was up to my elbows in suds and resentments over the pile of dishes I didn't use, but were left for me to clean. She invited me to the mall with her.

"The mall?" I shut the water off to hear her better. "Want to go somewhere else? I pretty much hate the mall."

I thought I'd make that clear since this first hang was the foundation of our friendship and I pretty much don't make a good mall buddy. "But I'd love to hang around with you. Wanna go walking?"

"Well, I'd love to go walking sometime but my mom-in-law got us pictures of Eli at Sears and I have to pick them up."

My heart sank. My breath became short. My lips and fingers numbed. That fast, a wound was opened.

How nice for you, I thought, that you have someone who gives a rip about you and your baby. A mom-in-law to pay for things like those dumb mall pictures that only grandparents really care about.

I was learning that I had not married into that kind of a family. That was writing that I should have seen on the wall way back at the Two-Birds drum circle beautiful wedding that Joe's mom almost boycotted because it didn't have a real priest. We'd *wanted* a real priest, but none would marry us, heathens that we were.

I was suddenly so jealous of this woman who wanted to befriend me. I wanted someone to want mall pics of my kids. And no one did. It was the challenge of my tragic loss, just like moms who've lost babies still get invited to baby showers. I had to live the life that was mine. Empty as it was, it was mine.

"Megan Pool, I like you so much that I will even go to the mall with you," I said.

And I did. Meg picked up Liam and me at around noon, swooping into our driveway in an older Ford sedan. She wore a stylish long sweater and had a giant travel mug of coffee in the cup holder.

"Thanks for picking us up," I said as I buckled Liam's rear-facing seat in the back next to Elijah. I gestured to her adorable outfit. "You look cute." I slid into the front seat and slammed the heavy door.

"Oh, thanks." Meg laughed. "I love this sweater. It covers everything I want covered, ya know. It covers a multitude of sins, girl. I'm definitely not back to my pre-baby weight."

"Feel that." I sighed.

"But, you know, I'm OK with it," she said, calmly backing out of our drive and into traffic. "Don't get me wrong. I'd love to get down again, but you know . . . there's just a lot of stuff I worry about more. I'm healthy so I thank God for that."

Holy perspective, Batman! What IS this girl? Is she for real?

The trip to the mall was relatively painless. I was broke, so I didn't have to worry about what clothes I could not look cute in anymore. All the short-shorts and mini-dresses wouldn't fit in our thin budget even if I could slip then over my widened hips and dimpled thighs. Picking up the pictures was a snap and then we sat down to nurse the boys and chat.

"So, tell me about yourself," Meg said, with the kind of smirk that showed she knew just how cheesy that opener was.

I laughed back in recognition of the cheese. "What do you want to know?"

"I don't know. Your deal?" The mall music echoed as Meg twisted open a water bottle and with a big swig asked, "What's your deal, Shannyn Caldwell?"

There was that crinkled up nose again. Meg had a cute nose. Little, upturned. I thought it might be Irish.

"Um . . . my deal?" I looked over my shoulders, left and right. Nope, she was talking to me.

I took a moment to think which part of my deal I felt it was time to share. "My deal is I'm a radio chick. I work for Magic 105.1 as a disc jockey. I work at Starbucks for insurance and coffee."

"Amen, girl." Meg laughed. And then she waited.

"I'm a yoga chick . . ."

"Really?" She sounded like she'd never met a yogini before.

"Yep." I gently laid Liam over my shoulder to burp him.

"Hum...I've always wondered about yoga," she said. Suspiciously, I thought. "What do you like about it?"

I looked for the nearest exit, just in case she was about to get overly church lady on me.

"Well, it helps me feel strong," I said. "And it's great for my organs and detoxing. I've got digestive issues and it helps with that." Liam let go of a giant belch. "No digestive issues for HIM!"

Megan did a spit take with her mug of water, spraying a fountain on the shiny mall floor. Our laughter bounced off the echoing wall. I took a deep breath and prayed the next truth would not become a sticking point for my new friend.

"Plus, it helps me open up, you know in other ways. I feel peaceful when I practice. I feel closer to God."

Looking into Meg's hazel eyes I could tell she was processing something. I was hoping that she was not going to come at me with something about how yoga was evil or whatever. I didn't take her for "one of those Christians" but . . . ya never know.

"What's your relationship like with God?" she said finally.

"Me? Mine? It's great. It's one of the best parts of my life. I thank God for my relationship with God."

We both laughed and switched sides for our babies. I appreciated how deep she was going and how quickly she was going there. I just hoped she wouldn't pull out a *you're going to hell* pamphlet next.

"Hum . . . so how do you talk with God?" Meg said when Eli was settled in. "How do you know it's Him? I mean, obviously, I'm a Christian and so I read my Bible, but how do you? I'm curious about that."

Her tone was genuine, not judgy, so I tried to be careful and choose words that wouldn't hurt or offend her. It was like walking in a field where bombs were buried. I chose my steps, pausing after each word to listen for a rumble of danger.

"Well," I said. "Prayer. Meditation. Yoga. Nature." So far, so safe. "It's all God. Everything."

Her eyes closed to near slits.

Retreat! I thought. It's a live one!

"And do you think of God as good or loving?" she eventually asked.

"Oh, totally. Absolutely."

I took a swig of my lukewarm coffee so I could assess the damage. Looking down, I realized little Liam had drifted off to sleep and so I swaddled him in his little flannel blanket and laid him on my lap.

"Isn't he beautiful" I said, falling deep into the softness of his baby skin and hair.

"He is. He's so cute, Shannyn." Meg leaned in for a closer look, "I think he looks like Joe. What nationality is Joe's family, anyway?"

"Irish. 100%."

She squinted, and I realized she was trying to find a way to speak without hurting ME. "Now, you lost your parents in a tornado, right? Do I remember that right from the party? You know, the Pampered Chef party. I think they'd just died."

Oh boy, here we go, I thought. I have to unpack this stuff again. I will always and forever have to explain a freaking nightmare every time anyone ever wants to get to know me. I could feel my nerves catch on fire, my brow furrow, my breath shorten. I quietly lay Liam into his carrier next to me on the bench so my silent emotional tide wave didn't wake him from a peaceful dream.

"Yeah. Wow, you have a good memory. They died in 1999 so it's been a while. Coming up on 7 years. Crazy."

"How are you doing with that?" she asked, casually.

Obviously, I didn't scare her. *She* didn't look for the exit. I felt like I was at my therapist's, with this probing. She looked at me, straight in the eye. That was refreshing, but honestly, couldn't we talk about "The Bachelor" or manicure trends or baby toys? This conversation was starting to hurt.

Evidently not. "It's hard. It sucks, but it is what it is. So . . ."

With a sigh and a shrug I showed her my white flag was up. I was clamming up. My jaw felt like it was wired shut. Like if this conversation continued, my tears and screams would echo off the walls instead of laughter and the mall cops would come and lock me into a padded room or show me the door.

She closed her eyes without saying a word and with her eyes still shut, pulled little Eli out from her blanketed shoulder and began to pat his tiny back. She knew I was broken. She knew.

"Do you have a Bible?" Meg said.

Uh-oh. I reached into my bag to check the time on my phone. "Me? Yeah. I think I have one. I'm sure of it. A lady gave it to me once. I was her waitress. I think I even know where it is."

I was only half joking as I rubbed sanitizer on my hands and offered some to Meg.

"No thanks," she said as Eli let his burp. "Good job, buddy," she said kissing him on the squishy cheek. "I want to buy you a Bible. Will you let me do that? I insist. I really want to."

First she had me go to the mall and now I was gonna hunt down my Bible? Who was this person?

She expertly snapped up her nursing bra and folded up the blanket from over her shoulder.

"You insist?" I'd never had anyone *insist* anything in my life. "Well, OK. Sure." I discreetly snapped mine too. "Man, I wish they made cute nursing bras!"

"A-MEN, girl!" Meg said.

How could we be so simpatico one minute and so diametrically different the next?

The bookstore was right across from us, so we packed up the boys and headed in. Our commonality extending beyond nursing boys, nursing bras and coffee, our shoulders both lowered from around our ears as we hit the silent whisper of paper backs and the reverence of café music in the speakers. I could tell Meg was in a cozy bookish happy place as much as I was.

She scanned the floor plan for the Bible section and led me there.

I was astonished by the selection. "Wow. I'll BE. There's a whole *section* for Bibles. Who knew!?"

"What kind do you want?" she said.

"Um…I have no idea? There are kinds?"

Meg pulled a couple off the shelves. I felt some covers to test for their comfort in my hand.

"Well, there is the King James, which is the old fashioned, fancy language. A lot of people find that one hard."

"Well, I'm also a Shakespeare freak, so I think I could hang." I opened a crinkly onion skin page and smelled the leather and the looked at the price. Yikes! $65! "What else is there?" I said.

"OK, so there's thing one called the NIV…New International Version. It's what I read. It's more user friendly for me. And then there's one that's a paraphrase in common language called *The Message*. There's actually a ton more."

She wasn't kidding. There were Bibles for teens and tweens and boys and men. There were ones for women that looked more like purses than books.

I started to get a panicky, overwhelmed feeling. It was bad enough to be in Bibleville, but now I had to pick a version? I couldn't breathe for a second. "You read NIV?" I said "Let's get that. That way if I have a question we have the same thing."

"Cool. Great." Meg pulled two black leather NIV's off the middle shelf. "Now one more question. There's the kind that has everything Jesus said in red letters. That's called "red letter Bible."

"Brilliant name," I said.

"Right?" Meg said. "Does that matter to you?"

Liam was starting to wake up, kicking off his little socks onto the carpet. I started to panic a little more. "Um, sure. Yes. That seems like a good idea," I said.

With that we selected my first Bible, a purse-sized black soft cover red letter NIV.

"It's really pretty," Meg said. She pointed out the gilded edges of the pages and the built-in bookmark ribbons.

"Yeah, it is. Thanks, Meg." We shuffled our strollers and diaper bags through the check-out labyrinth. "Where do I start? It's a really big book and I'm a really bad reader."

"You crack me up." Meg shook her head as she glossed her lips with something strawberry and then handed the teller her debit card. "Start with the Gospel of John."

"I really am a bad reader," I said. "I don't read big books. I like short form."

It was true. I couldn't put two letters together until my dyslexia was diagnosed in 5th grade.

But I decided it would be interesting to see what all the fuss was about with the Christianity thing. I mean, things with Joe were still a nasty mess of unpaid bills and blame. My heart was still shattered from the loss of my folks. And I was lonely. So I look the bait and started with the Gospel of John.

I poured a cup of black coffee and sat down on the couch in our front room. Even *that* made me feel totally church-lady. I could see how it was a slippery slope that might lead to quilting and casseroles and buying Jell-O molds.

My world was about to get flipped right over.

The Gospel of John! What was this stuff? Why didn't anybody know about this stuff?

That was what I thought as I soaked in the first few pages of John.

In honesty, on my first pass, none of the big stuff at the top really stuck out. None of the "In the beginning was the Word" stuff made a lick of sense to me except to say that this John seemed convinced something off-the-chain amazing was happening-something bigger than anything I'd read about in my yogic texts. Yogis and yoginis (girl yogis) swoon when master teachers come to town, making pilgrimages to sit at the feet of gurus who one by one fall from grace and leave their students with nothing but limber hamstrings and bitterness. The teachers tour like flexy rock stars with mala beads.

So, no, John's devotion was not what made this good news stand out as something that authentically happened. John didn't point to himself, he pointed to Jesus, his master. Jesus didn't even point to himself, but his Father in heaven. It was the details. I was blown away starting at John 1.

The next day Jesus decided to go to Galilee. He found Philip and said to him, 'Follow me.' Now Philip was from Bethsaida, the city of Andrew and Peter. He told this stuff like someone actually would if they were telling you. You know...she went to Ferndale and hung with Meg and Reba.

Philip found Nathanael and said to him, "We have found him of whom Moses in the Law and also the prophets wrote, Jesus of Nazareth, the son of Joseph." Nathanael said to him, "Can anything good come out of Nazareth?" Philip said to him, "Come and see." This went over my head. I didn't know anything about the law and prophets, except what I'd overheard from my Jewish friends.

Jesus saw Nathanael coming toward him and said of him, "Behold, an Israelite indeed, in whom there is no deceit!" Nathanael said to him, "How do you know me?" Jesus answered him, "Before Philip called you, when you were under the fig tree, I saw you." Nathanael answered him, "Rabbi, you are the Son of God! You are the King of Israel!" Jesus answered him, "Because I said to you, 'I saw you under the fig tree,' do you believe? You will see greater things than these." And he said to him, "Truly, truly, I say to you, you will see heaven opened, and the angels of God ascending and descending on the Son of Man." Now I was seeing Jesus in the same light as Paramahansa Yogananda.

He was a mystic guru, it seemed. Why don't people *know* Jesus is this awesome, I thought.

Then he did His first miracle: Water to wine. Go Jesus! I decided if I got to heaven, I wanted to taste that wine. Next he "cleansed" the temple. I'd never in all my days thought of Jesus as someone who could go Chuck Norris on you. But there it was. Jesus was not a wimp, at least not according to this John guy. He was hardcore. Who knew?

And then this happened in John 3:

Now there was a man of the Pharisees named Nicodemus, a ruler of the Jews (another seemingly accurate historic detail).

This man came to Jesus by night and said to him, "Rabbi, we know that you are a teacher come from God, for no one can do these signs that you do unless God is with him." I knew people who could do amazing things… not this amazing.

And then Jesus's next red letters blew my mind. Jesus answered him, *"Truly, truly, I say to you, unless one is born again he cannot see the kingdom of God."*

What? What the heck was that? I knew I better figure it out, because I was so, so over this life. I wanted to see the kingdom of heaven. Urgently. And so I read on.

Nicodemus said to him, "How can a man be born when he is old? Can he enter a second time into his mother's womb and be born?" Jesus answered, "Truly, truly, I say to you, unless one is born of water and the Spirit, he cannot enter the kingdom of God.

Oh, my God! *What* was He talking about? I had to figure this out.

That which is born of the flesh is flesh, and that which is born of the Spirit is spirit. Interesting. I was getting it. *Do not marvel that I said to you, 'You must be born again.'* Oh, good. It wasn't just me. *The wind blows where it wishes, and you hear its sound, but you do not know where it comes from or where it goes. So it is with everyone who is born of the Spirit.*

Wow.

OK . . . so I had to be "born again." Whatever *that* was. And then I came to John 3:16, the ever-famous football game and Today show crowd verse . . . *For God so loved the world, that he gave his only Son, that whoever believes in him should not perish but have eternal life.*

I could quote this one along. Almost every American probably can. But I had no idea what it meant. In the same way repetitive prayers can lose their life and become mind- and heart-less, Scripture must do the same thing, because I'd had John 3:16 splashed in my face millions of times. The salt must have lost its saltiness in the delivery, or God just hadn't removed the scales from my eyes yet, because until then people might just as well have been holding up a "Five-Dollar Foot Long" sign. It was words. I didn't get freedom's message in it. But that night I read on to: *For God did not send his Son into the world to condemn the world.*

What? Wait a second! I thought, He didn't?

But in order that the world might be saved through him.

Wow. Mind blown.

Whoever believes in him is not condemned. What? We are not condemned? *But whoever does not believe is condemned already, because he has not believed in the name of the only Son of God.*

Really? Jesus said that? OK....

And this is the judgment. Dum, dedum, dum, *the light has come into the world, and people loved the darkness rather than the light because their works were evil.*

Wowie. Some people do. Did I? What works was he talking about?

For everyone who does wicked things hates the light and does not come to the light, lest his works should be exposed. OK, right, yeah...

But whoever does what is true comes to the light. I wanted to do what was true. I wanted to come to the light.

So that it may be clearly seen that his works have been carried out in God.

I would have to noodle on this one. Then there went John with more of those *this thing actually happened* details.

After this Jesus and his disciples went into the Judean countryside, and he remained there with them and was baptizing. John also was baptizing at Aenon near Salim, because water was plentiful there, and people were coming and being baptized (for John had not yet been put in prison). This read like a true story. This was a true story!

And suddenly *I* had become a disciple of Jesus from Bethlehem who continued to kick tail and take names all through the book of John. Giving all that insight to that woman at the well. Healing that rich guy's kid from the town where the wedding was. Healing that beat-up dude at the pool and all the while taking no credit at all, but giving all the cred to His "Father in Heaven."

Don't even get me started on the feeding of the five thousand! As an under-employed barista with two kids, the idea of being able to multiply food! Shut up! Then He did the walk on water thing. It was cool to read how *that* played out. And I wanted to be able to rest in a storm like He did. I wanted to trust that much, but the world . . . it was hard and the storms could kill me. I knew that.

One had killed my family and I was having a hard time believing in a God who loved me when my parents' death certificate read, "Act of God."

I wanted that Jesus stuff. I wanted that freedom and I believed what He said. He said right there we could *all* do that. The guy the Christians were crazy for said we all could.

I trusted what he said. I believed it. I didn't like all of it, but I believed it and therefore I became what the Christians called "a believer." My light was turning on. I knew there was a God out there, always had. I thought Christianity looked more like a clique or a club, and not a very fun one, either. Who would have thought it was the real deal, that *it* was where the party was at?

But there it was, the good news. There was a way out. I didn't have to *earn* my way in. It seemed that according to Jesus, my eternal destination was not beholden to me getting it right, learning my lessons, or figuring it all out. According to Jesus, all I had to do was "believe in Him and the one who sent Him" and I was covered. It wasn't *if* I got to heaven, it was *when* I got to heaven.

How could it be that simple? And if it was that simple, why didn't everyone know about it? Why were we all talking about Karma and moon phases and spirit guides when the problem was already solved? Then life *could* be regarded as blessing and not some maniacal and lovely death trap where we all fooled ourselves and our kids that it was beautiful when we knew full well it was a wreck…albeit a sometimes lovely one.

The good news was flipping me out.

Could it be that the kingdom actually *was* at hand? If so, what did that mean? In one reading of the Gospel of John everything in this broken world and my ruptured life made sense…if not in the immediate, certainly in the eternal. I. Was. Saved. God had come for me in a cross shaped life boat and rescued me.

The Gospel became like a favorite song. I'd read it again and again, each time getting ever more excited as my favorite parts unfolded. And I didn't just read it, over and over, this book of John.

I meditated on it as I inhaled and exhaled.

I carried this new revelation to my yoga classes and my very inhales and exhales became a sacrifice…an offering to the Lord Jesus, for what he'd done.

As I picked and weeded my vegetable garden in front of our house I would remember the risen Lord being mistaken for the gardener by his own tomb and wonder how HE pulled weeds, way, way down to the roots.

It was one day when I was up to my elbows in tomato plants, meditating on the Garden of Eden, that Rebecca came striding over from across the street with a big glass of iced tea in her hand.

"Howdy, neighbor," she said and smiled and waved.

"Hey, girl," I said. "What's up?"

"Oh, just working on some paperwork for Monday, but I'm coming up for air and thought I'd see how you're doing."

Rebecca was an "uptalker." You know those people who go up in inflection at the end of every sentence? That was her. It was cute.

It also made me want to go down with my inflection, just to see if it would counteract the effect of the up. It didn't.

"I'm good," I said. "Just loving all this produce. How can you look at all this bounty and tell me there's no God?"

"I know, right?"

She sat on the wood bench by the strawberries and smiled, probably because I'd already taken the *let's talk about God with the seeker* bait without her having to even toss it.

"He's abundant," she said.

"Indeed. And He loves us so." I filled up my basket with Romas and set it aside so I could fill my apron with cherry and grape tomatoes. "Want one? They're super sweet." I tossed a cherry to Rebecca.

She was startled but she caught it.

"There's basil right there by your left foot it you want it," I said. "It's awesome with the tomatoes."

"Wow. Go, girl! You have basil, too?"

"Oh, we have everything-more than enough of everything. If you ever want anything from the garden, just come and get it. You don't even have to ask. For real, just help yourself."

Reba wrapped a basil leaf around her tomato. "Wow, that's so generous. Thank you. I may take you up on that." She popped the whole thing in her mouth with a Cheshire Cat grin. "Meg tells me you got your first Bible."

There was that up-talking again.

"I did." I said . . . down talking. "I love it. It's great. It's rocking my world."

"For real?" she said, practically spitting tomato seed in surprise "That's so cool, Shannyn!" It was like I told her I just got cast on Broadway. "What are you reading?"

"John. Just John so far." I poured out my apron into an empty mixing bowl and stretched my arms up to the sky to relieve my bent-over back. "I'm a super slow reader, but I love it. I love the Bible...that it's in bite-sized-pieces. That really helps."

I sat down on the wooden bench next to her. A bench Joseph had made.

"So, how are things with you and Joe?" she up-talks.

"Good." I up-talk, too. A lie.

"Good." Pause. Long one. "So, I wanted to tell you that if you have any questions about the Bible, I'd be happy to try to answer them. I'm no expert, but I read it a lot."

"Oh, thanks." I said. And I was sincere. "I'm good so far. I think when I'm done with John, I'll just reread it. It's a pretty deep book. There's a lot in there that I don't want to skim over, you know." I dusted the dirt from my knees.

"It is. No doubt. I love John. Jesus called him John the Beloved." Reba eyes were twinkling.

"Cool," I said. But I could feel the evangelical sights closing in on me. "I'm good for now. But if I have any questions for you I will ask. Promise."

Down-talking. Very. I thought that was enough of a signal that I was *done* talking, but Rebecca obviously did not pick it up. She pressed on.

"How's your heart, girl? You've been so on my mind." She slid right up next to me and took my grimy hands in hers. "Can I pray for you?"

"My heart? How's my heart?" My guard came up like the force fields on the Starship Enterprise. I wished for a cloaking device, too. "My heart is broken. My heart is broken. Shattered, OK? I am sad." I stated them as the cold, dry facts they were. "I wish that I could just fill out a box like kids do at school. 'He's allergic to peanuts. She has an inhaler. This one has a broken heart.' That's just how it is."

I got up from the bench and brushed the dirt from my bum. I squeezed the trigger on the hose and washed my hands. "You know about my parents, right? Have I told you? My parents were killed in a tornado."

Her amber eyes locked to mine. I could see her genuine compassion.

"My heart...well. I don't expect it will ever be OK again. Thanks for praying. I'll take all the prayers I can get." Down...talk.

"I'm so sorry, Shannyn. I'm so sorry." Reba's brow was deeply furrowed. You could have planted a row of corn between her eyes. "But that's what Jesus is for."

"With all due respect," I said, "I honestly hope and pray I never think like you. Jesus...the answer to everything. Jesus is awesome. I love Him. I had no idea how cool He was. He's rad and I follow Him." Good God, I think, so I'm saved and they *still* feel like they have to save me? What the...? "I hardly think He's the answer to everything. It's kind of silly. Jesus . . . came so my heart wouldn't be broken? My heart would be broken with or without Jesus, I thought. But I love John and I love Jesus and I love you."

Again, I thought I'd put the end to our conversation. Again, Rebecca had more to say.

She gave me a tight-lipped grin, the laugh lines around her eyes making an appearance in the noonday sun. "OK. OK. If you ever want to talk or pray . . . I love you, my friend."

She was shaking my hands like a grandma does with a three year old when she's giving important instructions. She rose from the bench and reached for her now empty iced tea glass.

"I love your sunflowers," she said. "They're awesome. They look so cool from across the street. You bless us so much with them. You bless the whole neighborhood with this garden."

That was a bunch of Christianese but I got it. I said, "Thanks," and got up and sprayed cool water in my mouth from the hose. Looking up, I expected to see Reba half way across the street, but she was still right there.

"You should come and sit on the porch with me some time," she said. "And you're always welcome to home group, ya know. It starts at 6 on Wednesdays. There's always food and kids are totally welcome."

I did love the idea of not cooking once a week.

"I just may take you up on that sometime," I said. I snipped a branch from the sunflower and passed it to her with a smile. "You should take this."

"THANKS!" she said with her biggest voice.

She swept through the garden and crossed back to her house, and I picked up the shovel to thin my carrots realizing full well that Rebecca was the one tending the garden that day.

CHAPTER 7

THE WORLD'S BEST MYSTIC PIZZA

Father, open up the floodgates of your goodness and your healing power in my heart and mind. Where there is still brokenness, I pray that you would reveal it to me and walk me through it to the other side. Thank you for what you have done and for what you continue to do.

I wasn't surprised when Meg gave me a call the next day just to see how I'd been. I knew that I was now officially a church lady project.

But I didn't mind because I liked these Christians. They were unlike any Christians I'd met. They were joyful and gentle and didn't want to talk about politics.

But part of me did wonder at what point they would stop trying to evangelize me to their way of thinking, realize I WAS a follower of Jesus now and start to talk to me the way they *must* talk privately with one another about awful sin or the crime against God that our country had become.

I thought we all knew how Christians think. These particular ones were just really good at not showing it. It did not occur to me in any of our encounters that they just liked me and wanted to be my friend. I was convinced they wanted to win souls for Jesus, although I'd never heard those words before, not from them. I just knew that's what the deal was.

But when Meg called to see how I was a couple of things happened that just plain blew my mind.

First, she offered me a plate of brownies that she "had to get out of her house, dude, before she ate them all."

"Girl, I feel you," I said. "Brownies are the bomb. I'm still trying to lose baby weight here, but I'm sure Joe and his friends will love them."

I didn't know why, but I was surprised that the super spiritual Megan still cared about fitting in her jeans even though she did not find her *value* in her jean size. I was relieved to learn she still lived in the same universe as me.

While we were talking, Meg's call waiting went off.

"Shannyn," she said, "can you hang on real quick? I'll get right off. I'll be right back, promise."

She clicked over and as promised was right off with no word of the caller on the other line, who turned out to be my brother, Ryan, calling to thank her for buying me a Bible and modeling Christ for me. I know it was him because *he* told me so, when he called me later that hour. Meg never said a word about that call being Ryan and to me that was such a testimony to her ability to keep matters private. There was not one gossipy bone in her body, or it would have surely been exposed that minute. Clicking back, you'd think she'd say "OMG! YOU'RE not going to BELIEVE who that was!" but instead she said, "So...how do you like the Bible? Are you still in John?" What kind of a person was this?

"I'm loving it, girl. It's rocking my world."

"That's so awesome, Shannyn! It's so cool to see what God's doing in your life! I praise God for that."

So much Christianese and so much excitement!

"So do you think you're going to go to small group across the street?" Meg said. "You know it's Wednesdays and that you are so totally welcome, right?"

"Yeah, yeah," I said. I decided that I better do some dishes and turned the water on to fill the white ceramic sink. I needed a distraction from the full court press. "I'm not sure. Maybe. That's about the time Joe gets home from work and I feel like I never see him, so . . . sometime."

"Oh, totally. Whenever, you know? Just want you to know you're welcome. And you know when our church meets, right? Sundays at the senior center. 5:30 pm."

"Oh, evening? Sunday night? Wild." Who'd heard of a Sunday night church?

"OK..." Meg laughed. "I guess it's wild. We have pizza! Now that's wild."

She laughed harder. I loved her laugh. It was the opposite of a courtesy laugh or a radio laugh. It was real and it made me want to laugh, too.

"Really? Pizza? At church? On Sunday night. You GO, Meg Pool. Now THAT we'd love to check out some time."

Double score! Brownies and a Sunday without having to cook! I could get behind this plan. Joe might even go for it, too. They were trying to get me to buy in, like Avon or Amway, but this seemed to have a much bigger pay off, and the pyramid might be non-existent.

It was a hot August Sunday evening the first time we went to a real live Evangelical church. Beyond the pizza, what we were fed was the most affectionate connection between a man and his maker I'd ever seen.

It was simple. It happened around card tables in a rented room of a senior center tucked back in the grassy corner of a Royal Oak neighborhood. There were about 16-18 people there.

A 40-something single guy with grey hair sat next to a late-teens couple. They were adorable, her in a flowery shirt and t-shirt, him in cargo shorts and Birkenstocks. An artsy looking 40-ish waif of a girl swept up to say hello.

"Hi! How are you? I'm Noreen! Have you been here before?"

I was wondering if she was just uber-friendly or a greeter. Joe picked greeter.

"No. We've never been here before." He had his Marine voice on.

"Well, welcome!" She smiled and I decided Joe was right: definitely greeter.

"Your baby is so cute! May I hold him" She opened her arms wide.

"No, that's OK," Joe said, "We can hold our child."

His whole countenance changed when he was in military mode. He was focused-pressurized.

Oh boy, I thought, not everyone understands his rough delivery.

But her bronzer sparkled as she laughed away the tension. "No problem! So how did you hear of us?"

"I'm friends with Megan Pool," I said quickly before Joe gave another Marine Corps response "We're baby/mama friends."

"Oh, that's great. Meg is great."

Noreen sparkled in her eyes too. "Did you know Meg's preaching today?"

"What? Did you say Meg is preaching? For real? Wow, that's so cool!"

I smiled and as I did, a bald dude in his 20's strummed an acoustic guitar. It was Nate, the home brewer from the party. They all went silent.

"Lord, we love you and we thank you for your presence here today," he said in a gently reverent voice. "Have your way in this place. In Jesus' name. Amen."

Everyone said "amen" except Joe, who whispered too loud: "They let women preach in this church."

I looked around to make sure no one heard. "Shhh," I said, eyes exploding from my skull.

It *was* wild, though. They let women preach. I did not recall ever seeing such a thing. And it wasn't some puffed-up woman in a suit with helmet hair. It was Megan, dressed in her blue jeans, clutching her travel mug. If Meg was a Barbie, she would come with a coffee cup and a Bible.

As everyone was opening their eyes from the brief prayer Nate strummed his guitar again and began to sing some song I'd never heard.

Light of the World

You stepped down into darkness

Opened my eyes

Let me see

They all closed their eyes again. I kept mine open and saw Meg up front. Rebecca was touching her head. I could tell she was praying for Megan. The cute little hippie couple had their hands raised all the way up in the air.

Beauty that made

This heart adore You

Hope of a life

Spent with You

Since then I've learned that there is a Christianese usage of the word "corporate" which means doing something as a group, so…if you are praying in a group it's called "corporate prayer." If a bunch of you are singing songs together, that's *corporate worship*. I tell you there is a learning curve in the transition from "the world," which is also

Christianese for any one or thing that is not Christian. *The church* is the lingo for the tribe of people who follow Jesus.

I watched Noreen, eyes pinched shut, singing her heart out. Her corporate (in the business man sense of the word) husband, in his uniform of blue dress shirt and khakis softly closed his eyes, too. It was a lot like deep meditation, I thought. Like SRF a little, only these people stood and sang instead of sitting and chanting.

Noreen's husband's hands were also out, like he was holding a watermelon or something. He was obviously singing from the heart and I wondered if his co-workers could ever picture him this open, this vulnerable. And as they sang, Rebecca finished her prayers over Meg and joined in the singing. Right where she was, she fell to her knees, closed her eyes and raised her hands high in the air.

Here I am to worship

Here I am to bow down

Here I am to say that You're my God

So, they were singing to their God. OK.

You're altogether lovely

Wow. They really liked Him. Never heard of a lovely God, but . . . OK.

Altogether worthy

But what was THAT?

Altogether wonderful to me

That was so sweet. They really loved him. They really seemed to *know* him.

King of all days

Oh so highly exalted

Glorious in Heaven above

"Blab la blab la blab la blab la blab la bla" It was way too much Christian code. Missed it.

Humbly You came

To the earth You created

What a minute! What?

My gears started turning. Yes . . .humbly . . . into earth….He created. Wow.

All for love's sake became poor

I was about to flip out. This was deep, deep stuff these people were excited about. I closed my eyes, too, and although I didn't know the words, I listened and agreed.

Here I am to worship

Yes.

Here I am to bow down

Yes.

Here I am to say that You're my God

He was my God? I thought he was my savior, my guru, but my *God?* I couldn't say that yet.

You're altogether lovely

Yes.

Altogether worthy

I guess that meant that his death on the cross was enough to cover me, so . . . Yes.

Altogether wonderful to me

Absolutely.

And then Nate really turned up the heat with his strumming and everyone got even more intense. Noreen was crying. Her hubby was doubling over, his blue oxford bending toward the pleats in his pants. Joe and I gave each other the *What's going on here?* glance. The *this was a little like a spectator sport,* glance. Then the *do you think we're in danger? Should we go?* glance.

But I looked to Meg, whose hands were extended straight up like the rabbit ears on old-school TVs and then to Joe, whose eyes were *not* closed meditatively. We silently decided to wait it out. And they sang on.

I'll never know how much it cost

To see my sin upon that cross

They were shouting it to the Lord. They were wide open. All in. Whatever it was they were experiencing, it was *real* to them.

I'll never know how much it cost

To see my sin upon that cross

It was a lyric I still didn't truly comprehend, and I knew Joe didn't either. A lyric which, in honesty I am still not convinced anyone can understand. But they clamored to understand and to confess and to repent.

Now every hand but ours was raised right there in the back corner room of an otherwise empty senior center. No other lights in the building were on. In just this one room the light was shining so brightly it was blinding. It was sunshine on bright white snow. It sparkled.

Here I am to worship

Here I am to bow down

Here I am to say that You're my God

You're altogether lovely

Altogether worthy

Altogether wonderful to me (3)

And I wanted love like that. I had yearned for it from my earthly father. I had searched for and expected to find that kind of love in my husbands. I'd tried to find that kind of love—that altogether lovely, worthy, wonderful, exhausting, expansive, all-encompassing love in my friendships, my yoga and meditation. I'd tasted love as I desired it but found it more like fireworks than the all-consuming fire these people were clearly caught up in. I wanted it. I wanted to catch on fire and burn and that's exactly what happened.

It was like a water slide...the way you creep up the dizzy staircase with the echoes of shouts from the deck below. Your heart thumps in your tongue. You poise at the top and just as the lifeguard puts his hand on your back to give you the all clear to go and you think, "I can't do this...this is crazy!" You let go and with a WEEEEEEE and AHHHHHHH you ride the wave through its twists and turns and even its bumps until you land with a victorious splash in the pool at the end.

It was like that. These people had walked me up the slide and now...I was...well....what exactly was I?

CHAPTER 8

THE BREAKDOWN/BREAKTHROUGH

*Thank you Father, for your abundance and help me to remember
it when I feel that I'm lacking. Root me deeply into yourself so that this
is not just a Healing Season, but a healed woman.*

One of my first thoughts was: Oh, no! I'm becoming one of them.
How many shades of crazy am I going to turn now?

But I couldn't help it. I couldn't deny it. It was truth. Jesus Christ
did die on the cross as atonement for my sin. He *rose* from the dead.
Sin=forgiven. Problem=solved. Then He hung out with His peeps
because He loved to. And continued to teach (which He still does)
and then ascended to the Father in heaven. Plus, He is coming again
to set things right once and for all.

He was real and alive and had set me free. If that meant that I had
to become one of them...then so be it. Plus, Meg and Reba and Jim
and a bunch of the folks from the church...they seemed like one of
us, not one of *them.*

I mean no offense to anyone, so allow me to unpack that. I've
witnessed in the church before my conversion, a priest who would

not baptize my baby because she was born out of wedlock. The same priest also said that if my daughter wasn't baptized, she'd go to hell. See the problem there? We all have stories like that.

I witnessed many countless, angry people screaming on the street about repentance and they came as carnival sideshow hawkers selling fear, not freedom.

We all have stories about the judgmental church lady who snubbed us. If we didn't, Dana Carvey would not have so strongly resonated with us as he pinched up his lips with the classic, "Well, isn't that special?" It was hilarious because we all knew that lady…and she had hurt us.

But growth takes risks and I wanted to grow in Christ. I wanted to know Him deeply. I wanted encounters with Him of the degree that I'd experienced meditating at the SRF gardens in Cali. I wanted to know Him, His character, His will, His heartbeat and voice. I wanted to feel Him breathing over me and stilling me in my chaos. I wanted more than the momentary cultivated peace that I gleaned on my yoga mat. I wanted it all…and according to my little Bible, I could have it.

And now, nothing was going to pry the Lord out of my heart. He was my life raft. I needed Him to live. Without the cross I was sunk. I needed His word to show me how to live. And so, I took one of those risks of growth and went to my first ever old lady Bible study.

That's how Megan pitched it to me a week or so after the worship service. "Hey, I don't know if you'd be interested, but I go to this old lady Bible study at this church in Troy on Tuesdays. If you'd ever want to come with me, I'd be happy to pick you up."

An old lady Bible study, I thought. I am surely losing my cool. But I somehow couldn't resist. Maybe it was the free child care. Liam was still not sleeping through the night and I was truly losing my mind from lack of sleep. Or it could've been the promise of free coffee and dessert every week. Or simply the longing to spend time with women that were about the age Mom would have been.

Whatever it was, I bit and we went.

Meg picked me up with her customary travel mug of good coffee at about 8:30 am. That felt a little early for my taste, but it was like a field trip, I thought. I got to go and see the Bible study, a live-in-a-real church Bible study. I wondered how they would deal with me, if they would even look at me. If they would pretend to be nice to me, or if they, too, had what Meg had, what I'd just found: a Savior who calls himself love. Oh, how I hoped for the latter.

"Meg, just so ya know," I said, digging in my messenger bag for a mint, "I'm just checking this out. Don't feel like you have to rearrange anything to pick me up each week."

I was already buying myself an exit strategy in case it was a nut fest.

She pushed a button on her radio. "Dude, I totally know that. You so don't have to come if you don't want."

"No, I want to come. I just want to check it out, ya know? This whole thing is super unexpected to me. Mint?"

I passed the Altoid tin her way. She waved it off.

"Oh, come on," I said. "They're curiously strong."

Just then I noticed that Meg had landed on a radio station that instantly sounded Christian. The female host said something about needing to pray on a thing she was going through, and her co-host laughed along and said "Amen."

"What's this station?" I asked.

"Oh, I'm not sure. I think it's Family Life Radio. I like them."

"What? For real?" How did I not know that there was Christian radio…that sounded like…radio? It was great, though, because it confirmed that it was not just Meg and Jim who prayed about their problems as a way of solving them. Other people did it, too. Like Dawn, on the radio. Baffled, I stared out the window at the cars rushing by on I-75 North. "So, there's Christian songs?" I was flipping.

Meg laughed again. Her white teeth amazed me considering the amount of coffee she slammed. "Girl," she said, getting her swag on, "there is Christian just about everything. There's even Christian MINTS!"

"Shut UP!" I wailed.

"Yep. They're called Scripture Mints."

"Who knew?" I said with a well now *that's* over the top tone.

The boys were starting to fuss. She checked them out in the rear view mirror.

"The natives are getting restless," I said.

"We are almost there, babies," she said in an enviably sweet mommy tone. She must be getting sleep, I thought. To me she said, "I think it's so cool what God has been doing in your life, Shannyn." She smiled, unveiling her lovely laugh-lines. Now I even envied her wrinkles! 20-something wrinkles are cuter, I thought, than 30-something wrinkles.

"I do, too. What a relief!" Not to sound cliché, but I sighed as if the weight of the world had been lifted off my shoulders. Indeed… it had!

"Right?" she said.

We laughed together. Now my laugh matched hers. Genuine.

Just then, we pulled off the freeway and quickly turned down an almost invisible road which according to Meg led to the church. This church, whose parking lot was full of neatly dressed ladies who looked like they ironed their clothing. I just prayed, Lord, why am I here? With a deep breath, I unclicked Liam from the back and walked in the door.

It was, in fact, an old lady Bible study. A Beth Moore study, to be exact… *Breaking Free.* The median age of the group was probably 65 or 70, but there were several women in their 80's and one tiny wisp of a gal was 89. She shuffled across the gym-like room where we were signing up for the study with a plume of cotton candy white hair and a ruffled red collar on her blouse. She wore a blouse…definitely not a shirt.

She had a Bundt cake, drizzled with frosting, on a platter. "Where should I bring this, dear?" she asked of a gal who looked to be in charge.

"Just over there." The other woman pointed with pink pearled nails and a matching lipstick smile.

"Are you good?" Meg whispered to me under her breath. She could probably feel me freaking out.

"Girl, I'd pay money just to see that old woman," I whispered back. "I'm good."

And that was true. I didn't come with expectations. I just came, and I was already blessed by it. It was our turn at the registration table now, and I decided to bite the bullet and sign up. I felt, for lack of a better term, the Spirit leading me. And so, even though Joseph and I had less than $200 in the bank, I chose to pay the $15 to get the book and take the class on *Breaking Free.*

There was a workbook and videos and a discussion guide, none of which I followed at all. I did not have time for homework. I was beat and burnt and spent and could barely get past Beth Moore's (one of my favorite teachers now) Southern gospel dialect and deep, deep Christianese.

But I loved being around Meg and the old ladies. I loved our teacher, Dorothy—most especially. Dorothy. What were the odds that my old lady Bible teacher would be named for a character out of the *Wizard of Oz*? I knew there was a God-wink in that and so I stayed the course and came Tuesday after Tuesday.

I got creamed in Fastest Fingers, a Bible study game where you're given a chapter and verse and the quickest one to look it up gets a prize.

"OK, Ladies, are you ready?" Dorothy would say in her command-ingly gentle voice. "Up for grabs today, a lovely-three tube sampler of the Clinique Spring perfumes!"

The women ohhhed and ahhhhed around the table as they drew their Bibles near.

"Now, don't get too excited. They are, as I say, only those little tiny samples, but they are lovely, I tell you. Lovely. And it's important that we do things to make ourselves feel lovely, girls."

I loved that she still called this aging cluster "girls." There was lightness in it. Not as heavy as "women," not as demanding as "ladies."

She smiled, clicking a star mint behind her teeth, and tucked a pen in behind her gold-hooped ear. "Fingers at the ready." Her green eyes twinkled, the perfect fit for her very tidy dyed-red hair. "Your verse is…"

The tension built like the announcer on Price is Right was about to shout "A new CAR!" Instead it was darling Dorothy saying "Proverbs 31:30! GO!"

Instantly, the most Midwestern of the ladies, a lanky short-haired woman in her 50's shouted, "I got it!" She was wearing a shirt, not a blouse. It neared manly dark blue, collared and crisp. Her sleeves practically crunched as she lowered her arm back down to a sea of delayed "I got it's!" But Dorothy heard and called on her.

"Yes, Jean?"

Jean straightened herself in the folding chair and read, "Charm is deceitful and beauty is vain, but a woman who fears the Lord is to be praised."

"Yes, and amen to that!" Dorothy said emphatically as she passed the tiny gift bag in Jean's direction.

And I thought, What? What did that just say? I need that! And these old people probably sure need that.

"What was that verse? I whispered to Meg.

She leaned in and opened my Bible to the verse without even really looking down.

"Now girls, have you heard of this book *The Purpose Driven Life* by Pastor Rick Warren?" Dorothy looked for confirming glances. "Girls, I tell you it is just fantastic!" She had a little Southern thing going, too. Maybe Florida… "And it is getting tons of buzz out there. Well, we will get to our prayers and praises in just a moment, but I want to tell you that today, *everybody* gets a prize because in addition to this wonderful study we are working on with our dear Beth Moore, girls, the other day I was at Costco and what did they have but an entire table of that book from Pastor Warren and I tell you the Spirit of the Lord spoke to my heart and told me to get one for each of you here today!"

The girls all golf-clapped as Dorothy passed down book after book to the tables . . . even to me. My heart remembered Christmas, the ornaments, basement and prisoners. Breaking Free, indeed. I loved the book cover: burgundy brown with a cream colored oak tree drawn on the front.

"What on earth am I here for?" it said. Good question, I thought. Plus, the cover art matched my house and with Joseph being the tree man that he was, I decided to leave it out on our nightstand . . . where it sat, unopened.

Expectations are a funny thing. In one way, they drive us, keep us on track. In another way, they steal from and sabotage our joy.

I had expectations of my walk with God. They were being met and exceeded. Between the sweet timelessness of the Tuesday Bible study, the comfort and fun of the Wednesday night group at Reba's and the communal connection of the Sunday service, I was becoming truly immersed, marinated in the Christian way of living. Prayer was becoming my everything. Now that I knew Him, I could simply come to Him and tell Him what I needed.

And what I needed . . . it was peace. I had little, if any at all, left. Joseph and I were still fighting. We fought over money mostly—the lack thereof.

One day as autumn was closing in and the garden stopped providing for our grocery bills, I reached my breaking point and I screamed at my husband. The kids were at the park with a neighborhood "big kid" and with the freedom of an empty house I turned my volume all the way up in hope of getting the anger out to stay.

"I WORK! EVERY DAY! And we still can't PAY THE BILLS! Why don't you HELP ME!"

Joe shouted back. "Why don't I help YOU?" His brow knit together like stiches between his eyes. "Why don't you help YOURSELF, lady? Or better yet, ask your imaginary friend!"

"Imaginary friend?"

"Jesus! Why don't you just ask HIM for the money to pay the bills? Why don't you ask Him, while you're at it, to show you how to clean a HOUSE! This place is filthy!"

"I clean EVERY DAY!" I yelled back.

Joe kicked the "filthy" dining room chair. It was now a brawl.

"YOU CLEAN!" I screamed, my hands raised high about my head, fingers clawed.

"ME! HA!" Joseph laughed a spiteful scoff as he tossed himself back on the couch and put his feet up "Learn your place, woman!"

Oh my GOD, I PRAYED. How did I get here? WHAT is going ON here? This was Taming of the Shrew. I HATED that play. Because Kate cracks, submits, gives up. Lame.

Lame. Lame. This could not be *my* story.

I planted my fists to my hips. "Don't you talk to me like that!"

"Shut up, woman," Joe, eyes locked on the TV, remote in hand "Haven't your Jesus friends taught you that yet? To know your place? It's all in your precious Bible."

"What are you talking about?" I truly was confused.

"You know why their marriages work? Because those men aren't married to crazy women like YOU! Their wives KNOW their place! Why don't you just quit your job and stay at home and have another baby?"

"Um…because I don't want to?" Now my breath was short. I softened my locked knees so I wouldn't pass out. "Because I want to work and we can't afford another baby because YOU DON'T WORK!"

I knew I was dealing a mean blow, but I said it anyway. I knew that Jesus was not the one who was talking. It was not Him…it was me, saved and still angry and bitter and broken. Why wasn't I fixed? What was the problem? Where was the peace? I didn't want to be like that street preacher who said he knew the truth and pointed fingers at everyone else. What was I becoming? What were *we* becoming? Where was the love we had…that we shared as we knew that God brought us together with that walk in the woods? He was the guy who brought my note.

He was the man who loved my strength and wanted to build me up, and was now ripping me limb from limb. And I was doing the same to him. But how could that sweet boy from the coffee shop who surely, I thought, blessed the people in his life, now be my biggest threat?

Joseph crossed his outstretched ankles on the arm of the sofa. "You're nothing, you know. You're never going to get another radio job now that they know you're crazy. Your own friends don't even want to be near you anymore."

This red flag flew high. I knew that true abusers will isolate and no matter how much I loved Joseph, I would not allow him to isolate me from my friends or from the church because without them I would surely fall off the cliff of unbearable despair.

"What are you talking about?" I whispered.

Quietly I sat down next to him on the couch. I practiced as much peace as I could muster, like when you're walking past a dog and you don't want it to attack. But attack he did.

"I'm talking about the fact they you are Coo-coo. Coo-coo. Coo-coo!" Joe repeated it like a clock at the top of the hour. "You are a crazy lady and I can't stand it anymore."

And just like that, he rose from the couch and marched up the creaky wooden stairs. I followed him to the closet where he was already pulling out his duffle bag.

"I need clothes," he said, and shoved some shirts and jeans and socks in the bag. "I need my guitar."

My breath became impossibly short – nonexistent. My head pulsed with fear. "What are you doing?"

"I'm leaving you, Shannyn," he said without even a glance my way, "It's over. Tell the kids I'm sorry….that I tried."

He spoke like a mean child on the playground. This was my best friend…and he was right: no one did want to hang with me anymore. I was alone and the prospect made me bury my face in my hands.

Here I am, again, I thought, ready to fall on my knees.

Don't do it, Shannyn. Don't fall.

I made my way back down to the green sofa, covering my head with the overstuffed pillows, trying to disappear. My very best friends, my thick and thin Jewish friends, had almost all slowly sneaked away from me and hidden themselves without a trace. It was generally a "back away slowly" retreat with the exception of one friend who told me that the Jesus thing "made me toxic" and that she "couldn't have me in her life." That I was a "vampire." The others were silent in their disconnection from me: not calling, inviting, returning calls. Theirs was a gentler retreat but a withdrawal nonetheless. My yoga friends were not in love with Bible-Shannyn either. Now it was mostly just me and Joseph and my new Jesus friends.

As I watched that best friend prepare to leave me, I knew I needed help. I was saved, but I was crashing off a cliff as fast as I did when John left and I lay in bed and cried out like a soldier in the trenches… "I'm wounded."

But this was the man "God had sent me." Why would He do this to me if He really did love me like the church people said? Like He said in my Bible? Why would he lead me to slaughter like that?

I stumbled to think straight but all I could do was beg. "Please, please stay. Please, Joe. Please."

His response: "It's too late now, Shannyn. It's over."

I flew to the lead glass front door like a firefly caught in a jar – so close to wonder, so close to being trapped. What if the kids walked home from the park and into this mess? As I scanned the horizon for those precious, innocent children that I had walked into this slaughter house of a family, I saw Jim and Megan pull into Rebecca's driveway.

There they were. My lifeline. The only thing that had every worked was prayer and I needed it now. I slid out the front door, undetected by the still-packing Joe. I felt like the woman with the issue of blood. I was desperate for an immediate action of the Spirit of God and the people who knew how to get Him on the phone were right there. I sprinted across the street, afraid they'd be gone before I could get to them. My knees were failing in the haste.

"MEG! JIM!" I shouted.

One door of the car cracked.

"Please, please, pray with me!" My voice lifted above the trees and bounced off the houses.

I was crying and crazed. I was flagging down Meg like a cop at a crime scene, "MEG!"

They looked busy, like this was meant to be a quick in and out stop, like they weren't even really planning on getting out of the car at all. But seeing me in my despair, Jim pulled the car to the curb, so I poured myself into the back seat. I was nearly hysterical.

Megan and Jim exchanged shocked glances. Meg turned herself around in her passenger seat to face me. "What's going on?" she said.

Jim looked back at me and then at Meg. It was an "I've got this" glance, "How can we pray?" he said.

"Please, please," I said. I was practically unable to put words together as I heaved in tears. "Just pray that I WANT the life I HAVE," I sobbed out. "Please, please pray for me to want my life."

Jim began to pray and I wish I could tell you what that prayer was, but in honesty I don't remember a word. I wept face down on the floor of the back seat and cried like a puppy who'd been left out in the wintery cold...lost...fearful...but not without hope.

"OH, GOD!" I cried out. "Oh, HELP!"

Meg extended her hand over my head and asked for the Father to send his peace to me and to Joe in Jesus name and I could feel Him descend. I felt the calm in the eye of the storm.

When Jim had said "amen," she asked again, "What's going on?"

"Joe hates me," I said. "He hates me. And he says he's leaving." I locked my eyes onto Meg. "What does the Bible SAY? What should I DO?"

She grabbed her Bible from her purse and began to play Fastest Fingers for no prize at all. When she looked up she said, "OK girl. And Jim, please feel free to jump in...but here's a question for you... is he willing to stay?"

"I don't know," I said. "He said he was leaving and I ran over here. He's packing. He could walk out right now."

"Where are the kids?" Jim said.

"They're at the park."

Jim nodded for Meg to go on.

"OK, because here is what it says in 1 Corinthians 7:13 'If any woman has a husband who is an unbeliever, and he consents to live with her, she should not divorce him. For the unbelieving husband is made holy because of his wife and the unbelieving wife is made holy because of her husband. BUT if the unbelieving partner separates, let it be so. In such cases the brother or sister is not enslaved." Megan tucked a black ribbon bookmark on the page and closed her Bible again. "So, again, do you have any idea if he would be willing to stay?"

"I don't know," I said. I was baffled at the truth of my response. How could I not know if my husband was willing to stay?

"We could ask him." Jim got out of the car and stretched his long arms to the sky. Then he stretched out each leg like he was limbering for a race. "Let's go ask."

And so, prayed up, and with my honorary big brother and sister, I bee-lined across the street where Joe was finishing a phone call, saying, "Thanks, man. I'll only crash there until I find a place. I'll see you soon."

I left Jim and Meg on the porch and stepped into the entry way. "Joe, I brought Jim and Megan."

I hoped he wouldn't explode, but instead, he was the opposite. Warm. Friendly.

Acting.

I opened the door wide and they both wiped their feet and came in. It felt powerful having clergy in my house. I felt protected.

"Hi, guys!" Joe said, gathering his bags and guitar into a pile by the stairs. "What's up?"

Jim took on the manner of military brotherhood. "Well, Joe, Shannyn says you're thinking of leaving and we wanted to know if you were willing to talk about that at all."

I was amazed at the way Jim diffused it. How it didn't sound "so bad" coming from him.

Joe tossed it off. "What's to talk about? It's irreconcilable differences. It happens all the time. We tried."

"Hum...hum." Jim often said that. Meg, too, as they took things in. "Well, one question for you."

"Sure, man. Shoot." Joe was so friendly, so cordial; it was maddening, like the only person on the planet that was hard to deal with was *me*.

"Were there to be a way to reconcile your differences . . ." Jim spoke softly, slowly, like Sherlock Holmes seeing past words into truth. "Would you be willing to stay?"

"Well, if there is a way to change this woman into something I would live with, I would sure want to know about THAT, I tell you." Joe was zipping up his duffle...looking for his jacket.

My lips were numb from anger. If I were to say what I wanted the house would explode. I dared not move them or they would catch like a match and erupt.

"OK," Jim said. "Understand, I'm not saying that the problem is you. I'm just saying...asking really... I know you're not happy..."

"You got THAT right, brother." Joe looked into the front closet and turned to Jim. "My coat isn't even where it goes. I bet you don't have to deal with that at your house, do you? I bet your wife makes sure it's where it goes."

"Why don't YOU make sure it's where it goes?" I was one inch away from kicking off my shoes and throwing down Jerry Springer style.

Meg grabbed my hand.

"OK...OK...maybe this is too much to work out today." Jim said. "In fact, I'm sure that it is, but just for now, Joseph, I'm wondering if you will answer that question." He tucked his hands into his jean pockets waited.

"What's the question, again?"

I was furious. Joe was messing with Jim now. So I was the one who answered, "Are you WILLING to stay?"

I wanted to pray, but I wasn't sure what to pray for. If he said "No!" I had a biblical get out of jail free card. If he said, "Yes," I was stuck, married to the man who was trying to destroy me. I held my breath and I waited too.

Joseph stopped his whirlwind of packing, planted his feat, locked a "feel me, bro" gaze with Jim and said, "I don't WANT to."

"It's a yes or no question!" I said. "Yes or no, Joe. Yes or no."

"Yes. I'm willing to." Joe ran his fingers through his hair like a drama queen. "But she's…"

"OK." Jim put his hand up like a crossing guard signals stop. "Thanks." He turned to me. "Now Shannyn, your husband says he's willing to stay."

I gave a sigh and a weary smile, half relieved, half exasperated. Meg gave me a gentle look that said she got it.

"I hate to say it, guys," Jim said giving his bangs of toss from in front of his glasses, "But we have to go. Let's try to do coffee next week and pick up here, OK?"

Surprised by the quickness of the exit, I just nodded.

"I'm so sorry but we're meeting people and we are actually already a little late," Meg said.

"You guys are gonna be OK," Jim said. "Don't freak out. You'll make it."

Meg hugged me. "I love you, friend. I'll call you tomorrow."

And they were out the door, with Joe behind them.

And I . . . I went upstairs to cry and listen for the kids' return from their playdate in the park, thankful that they were coming home to a quiet, albeit near-empty house.

There is pain whose arc is far too high for human words to touch. A pain that cries from deep, deep down in the canyon of despair. The wail of the mother whose child dies in war. The shocking terrorized cry of fathers in the streets after car bombs and drive-by shootings. The cry that makes the evening newsreel. The cry for help when no human help can ever come.

I cried like that as I hid myself beneath our deep red bedding, piped with gold – the bedding we'd picked out together. We'd conceived our beautiful boy in that bed and now it lay cold with the dream of our love, commitment, trust, kindness and every hopeful thing thrashed and beaten and left for dead with only one tiny heartbeat remaining.

"Yes. I'm willing to stay," he'd said . . . as he left. "Yes. I'm willing to stay."

Where was this "I'll never leave you" God that I was believing in? Why was He so hard to access? How could I get to Him?

I hoped He'd appear like He did to Saul on that Damascus road. I did not see him. I did not feel him, yet still...I hoped. I believed.

But I was scared. So, so scared. Not for me, so much, but for my kids.

"Oh God!" I cried out. "Oh, God! How could you do this to me? Why would you bring me to Joseph only to have him leave me? Why would you tease me with true love like that? Why? WHY? Why, GOD did you make us have a BABY? To bring HIM into this, mess. And my ALEX!!! My tears sounded like the cowardly lion. My ALEX. She deserves so much MORE. That's mean. You're mean. I don't understand you, God. I thought you LOVED me. I thought you..."

The sobs poured out like a broken dam that floods an unsuspecting city.

"I thought you loved me."

I heard the door open. I listened like an Indian with ear to ground. It was the kids, home from the park. I had to pull it together. Again and again and again I had to pull it together, but this time...I could not. I simply could not.

I lay in bed and sobbed as I heard Alex downstairs calling for us. "Mommy! Dad! We're home."

And for the first time ever, I could not get out a pretend "Hi, Honey." I couldn't get out anything. Not a movement. Not a peep.

I heard Alex's little footsteps dance up the spiraling wooden staircase. "Mom?" she called up in her tiny voice. "Mommy?"

Still I couldn't move, let alone speak.

She knocked on the door and cracked it open for a peek. With every bit of strength I had, I pulled the corner of the covers down enough to expose the top of my head. She'll think I'm napping, I thought.

And she did. "Sorry, Mommy," she whispered and pulled the door shut tight and then swept back down stairs to turn on the TV.

"Mommy's taking a nap," I heard her say brightly to her innocent little brother.

They were both unaware that their home was falling to tiny brittle pieces.

"I'm sorry, too," I said to no one there. "I'm so, so sorry."

And I wept and wept and wept some more, until I had no tears left. I didn't make much of a sound as I lay there alone thinking, "I'm so sorry, baby. I'm so, so sorry."

If it were not for those kids, and for the hope that kept me clinging in this life, I would have spun totally out of control. I would have gone finally and fatally mad, for sure.

I pulled hard on every single thing I'd ever learned in meditation practice. Closing my swollen eyes, I saw a picture . . . of a giant ball of yarn. It was tangled. Too tangled. I tried to stay focused on that yarn. To use what God showed me all those years ago at the ocean, to believe Him. To trust Him. To give over to Him. To get it straight.

And as I focused all of my mental and spiritual energy on trying to untie this knotted mess of a ball of string, trying to get it straight enough to knit in my mind's eye, I realized that that mess...it was my *life* and that I had created every single one of these glitches.

I tried to make something of the mess. But I couldn't. It was too big.

"I can't do it!" I said out loud. "It's too messed up. I can't fix it."

In my heart, I just lifted that mess of yarn and needles straight up to God in heaven. "I can't do it," I said to him.

And in that moment I heard the "still small voice." And here is what it said: "Be still and know that I am God."

I didn't know where in the Bible to find that, but I knew it was from the Bible. So now, He had done it again. First on the ground of the tornado, telling me "He is with me" and now here. He quoted the Bible and I knew. It was time. I had to take it seriously.

But . . . be still . . . and know you are God?

I knew that, I thought. I know you are God. I know that I am not, but I need *help*!

I lay in bed for hours and hours and hours and cried without sound or movement. I heard Joe come home. I heard Alex tell him I was sleeping. I heard him come upstairs and I braced myself for a tirade of abuse about how weak I was, but I was past the point of caring anymore.

Joseph entered the room quietly, but I didn't believe that meant he was going to be gentle with me. I tried to play sleeping or dead. I had absolutely nothing to give. Not a thing.

"Shannyn. Are you OK?" he whispered.

I didn't move. I didn't make a sound.

"Shannyn, are you losing it?" he asked.

I was scared to answer, but I knew I most certainly was completely losing it.

"Are you OK? You can tell me. Are you having a breakdown?"

He sounded sincere. Enough for me to eke out, like a balloon with too much air, "I'm scared."

"You need anything?" he said.

I shook my head. I didn't have any fight left in me. I didn't want to trust him, ask him for help, let him into my heart. I was in a desert, trying to find my way and my only guiding voice was the voice of God who seemed to speak in Bible, a language which I barely understood.

Joseph crept out of the room. Leaving me again, alone with my God.

What am I doing wrong? I cried out in my head to this invisible God of the Bible. What are you trying to show me? What am I supposed to learn? Help me. Show me. I need to learn!

And as my heart cried out, my gaze shifted to the bedside table and that book from Dorothy: *The Purpose Driven Life.*

I reached for it, surprised to find that my arm in fact did work. I pulled it under the covers with me. I hid. I knew…the baby, he'd want to nurse and I couldn't do it. I couldn't hold him. I couldn't. There was milk pumped in the freezer. These people, my little tribe of a family, would have to figure it out for themselves today.

The house sounded quiet. I wondered if anyone was home. I wondered, could the children feel, sense the eruption that just took place? Did they know it was all falling apart?

If I can't pull it back together, I thought, who will take care of them? My mom and dad, they're dead. It'll be Joseph for Liam and Alex will go back to her dad because there was just one blow that was too much for her dear mother to bear, and that blow was dealt.

I truly believed it might be the end for me. I wasn't suicidal like before, when staying well for Alex was all that held me together. I simply could not do it. It was over. The fat lady had sung and the only word she had for me was, "Be still."

And so I was. I was very, very still.

But how long could I maintain this? When would Joe come and rouse me from bed and tell me, "That's enough, young lady"? When would work finally call and ask when I'd be in?

Did I care? I did not. Not a bit, and that's what scared me most. I was slipping away. This was uncharted for me. I was utterly terrified.

I didn't know how long I'd been there. No one had checked on me in a long time. The sun, it seemed, was starting to go down. It must be 4 in the afternoon, 5 maybe, when Joseph cracked the door again to find me just as he'd left me, under the covers of what was once our lovers' bed. He handed me a card, tenderly kissed my forehead and left again, in silence.

I sat up and opened the card, a card which I still have. *We love you,* is all it said.

I knew that the kids needed me.

I knew almost nothing beyond that. I did not know what *I love you* meant coming from Joseph or anyone at all anymore.

I set the card down and picked up that book from Dorothy again. This time, I opened the cover and read the first words. *It's not about you.*

Wait...*what?*

It's NOT? Well then WHAT is it about?

I read on.

It's about God.

Wow, OK. Mind...blown.

If that was true. If it wasn't about me? What if God wasn't doing things *to* me, He was just...doing things. Then He did not steal my husband or kill my parents to prove some point to me. He did not do it *to me.* He just did it...because somehow, it was in His interest... His plan. The whole universe, not about me? To this child of the 70's that was a first time idea and in it, suddenly absolutely everything made sense. I know it sounds impossibly quick, so let me compare it to something that happened to me in High School.

I took Algebra and barely passed with a D. Then I took the required Algebra 2 and guessed on every single test, not understanding one word or concept our dear teacher presented. I was a "when in doubt, choose C" student all the way. Then, one day, near the end of my mandated tenure in the class, I looked up at a graph the teacher had drawn on the board and I understood it. Then she said something about the theorem she used to come to the conclusion and IT made sense too! All of the cumulative years of trying and failing suddenly shuffled the presented info into its right place, like a solved Rubik's Cube when the colors line up. I suddenly understood.

Now you may think, *Wow! What kind of a loving God would do that? Would kill my parents for His plan? How could that be? And maybe what happened to Shannyn is what happens to kidnapping victims who fall in love with their captors.* I know *right?*

I thought the same thing until right there in that red bedding with the gold piping. I remembered this Jesus who'd recently set my heart on fire. This Jesus. This Word made flesh. This Son of God. God Himself with human skin who suffered HIMSELF...who CHOSE to go to the cross to buy back my freedom. To reconcile me, my debt, bad choices, selfishness, fear, anxiety, bitterness, cruelty, self-abuse and the abuse of others. Me, who preached good news while screaming at her husband.

He too, I knew as I sat there in bed with the Purpose Driven Life pressed to my chest, He too had fears, but trusted his Father more than his fear. He had dreams, and I was sure that He surrendered and suffered greatly while doing so. He did not expect me or anyone to do what He was not willing to do Himself and He did it gladly... through His pain and His fear.

Because He totally and completely trusted His Father, our Father...He did it for the love of God and man. He died first. It was not so strange, then, that He'd ask me to do the same.

The blood of the cross flowed like a river though my bedroom that evening and the cloak of Christ laid out before me like gentlemen used to throw their capes on the mud for ladies to walk on. He asked me to follow Him. He made a way. It was His way. It was about Him. It was about the cross. It was about dying to what I wanted. It was about new life.

I was going to make it. I knew I would, because my life was not my own any longer. That time was come and gone. Now, I'd live and love and stay the course and try and try again. Now, I lived for Him.

Suddenly in that instant, my life…it had joy again. It had freedom beyond compare. The end game was certain. I knew where I was going when I died and what's more, this life, it wasn't a trap any more. I was back in the garden with my God. I stretched out an early morning stretch and flexed and pointed my feet, just to feel them again. I set bare toes, one by one onto the hardwood and went to my bedroom window.

Pulling back the curtain to let the evening light in my eyes I was shocked to find the sun was nearly set. I'd been there all day and evening, wrestling with the King, and I lost…which really, truly means I won.

The bite was back in the proverbial apple. It. Was. Finished. Hallelujah. It was done.

Now.

I could breathe again.

I emerged.

I felt like a shadow, not a person really. I felt transparent, thin, light, as I turned the squeaky faucet and splashed cold water on my face to refresh from the hours of weeping. A quick glance in the mirror revealed ever-deepening lines. It hurt. Have you ever cried so hard you felt like you just went swimming? Felt…wrung out like a sponge? Yep…like that.

I went downstairs anyway.

Joe sat in his armchair reading a paperback novel.

"Hi," I said.

"Sorry," he said softly. I knew he meant it. He uncrossed his legs and set the book aside. "How are you?"

There were those compassionate blue-green eyes.

I just shook my head from side to side. I still couldn't talk, but I was trying to imply that I was OK even though I couldn't make a sound.

Joe seemed to get the message. "Are you hungry?"

I thought for a minute. Was I…hungry? It was like he was speaking a foreign language. Was I?

I nodded.

"Do you want me to make you something?" He was a little urgent, like he was in sudden triage mode.

I myself couldn't quite even take the pressure of the questions and started to cry all over again.

This time, it was loud. I thought again, oh my, I am still cracking up. This is the point at which there is no return. I'm dust.

"OK…OK…it's OK." Joe rose from his chair and hugged me into his arms. I felt so small, weak. I was frail. I was vapor. He kissed the top of my head and backs of my hands. "What do you want to eat? Do you want Thai food?"

I cried even harder and shook my head at the thought of it. It was exhausting going to the mountaintop because, boy, that valley can beat you up. But what God said was true. What He told me that day as I struggled to walk and looked down to the ground in the wreckage and saw that glint from my daddy's walking stick and heard that still small voice. The same voice that had just told me to "be still and know" He said, "Though I walk through the valley of darkness and the shadow of death, I will fear no evil. For you are *with* me! Your rod and your staff, they comfort me."

The good shepherd, the Lord our God was doing what He said he would do, he was leaving the 99 lost sheep to come and get me! Now…for once and for all…I finally, *thankfully* had hope!

"Soup," I managed to get out.

"Soup," Joe said like I was Helen Keller. "You want soup?"

It was like I'd said the sweetest thing in the world.

"OK!" he said. "OK!"

CHAPTER 9

THEY'LL KNOW WE ARE CHRISTIANS BY OUR LOVE... AND OTHER STUFF.

God, be Lord of my mind and mouth. Let your daughter be a beacon of hope in the world and a reminder that because Jesus rose, there is hope. Be with me in hopeless times and send your wisdom. Live in me. You are welcome here.

H e took me to an Asian place for noodles and broth.

We ate in peaceful silence. Maybe we just talk too much, I thought. If we don't talk, can we fight? Not a worry for tonight, I told myself. Just nourish your body and enjoy the silence.

Then we picked up the kids, both of whom were at a friend's house.

"Hi, Mommy how are you?" Alex said as she hopped in the back-seat next to her brother who Joseph was buckling in.

"I'm good, baby," I said, and that was the truth.

The next day Meg gave me a call to see if I wanted to go to Bible break. I told her I didn't think that I could. That I was too exhausted. That I thought that I'd had a nervous breakdown.

"I don't know exactly what a nervous breakdown is," I said, "but whatever it is…I'm pretty sure I had one. It was scary."

And then I told her about the Rick Warren book and how I never realized that it wasn't about me and how everything made sense now.

"I'm sure you can call me born again. If before I was only saved, I am surely saved *and* born again or born again, again. Can you do that? Either way… it was brutal, my friend."

"That's so AMAZING, Shannyn!" Meg sounded like a tea pot ready to be tipped over and poured out. "That's so awesome! Can I tell Jim?"

"Sure…"

"Jim!" Meg yelled, "Shannyn says she got born again yesterday!"

"Happy Birthday, Shannyn!" Jim yelled in the background.

"Um…tell him I say thanks?"

"Have you told Joseph?" Meg said. She sounded like I got asked to the prom by the dreamiest guy in the universe.

"Naw," I said. "He's not too gung ho about the whole thing, you know. I don't know if he'd care much about the diff between saved and born again. He doesn't really want to talk about it and as much of a mine field as Jesus talk can be, I thought I'd just keep the peace going, know what I mean?"

"That's too bad. So, how did things go after we left the other day?"

"Um….I had a nervous breakdown, the end?"

"Did you and Joe work it out? Is he home?" It sounded like she was making dinner. Pots clanged. Cans were opened and emptied.

"Well…he apologized."

"He DID?! That's so awesome, Shannyn." A cabinet slammed. "That's really, really cool."

"Yep," I said.

And then I sighed a big, deep sigh because I knew that people who abuse have a cycle. It was not my first rodeo. I watched Dr. Phil (back when he was good). I knew the deal. 1-Be super mean. 2-Be super apologetic 3-Be super sweet 4- Swear to never do it again. 5-repeat.

I did not ever want to go back to the rage place. I feared I couldn't bear it. I had recent proof.

I think Meg either heard it in my voice or sensed it spiritually, because she said, "No problem if you don't want to come today, but I think it may be good for you. You know…we can get some ladies to pray with you, girl. You *need* prayer right now as you're going through it."

"Are you making dinner?" I said. "What are you making?"

I wanted to buy myself time to pray on it real quick.

"I'm just putting something in the crock pot. We're having company tonight and it's a super busy day, so…"

"Whatcha makin'?" I tuned my antenna, trying to pick up a message from the Most High as to whether I should brave the outdoors and try out my newly broken down born again self on the wide, wide world.

"Jerk chicken. It's awesome and it's the easiest thing in the world. It's crazy." I could tell she was running short on time. She sounded like she'd moved onto gathering jackets and getting shoes onto the child, "I'll give you the recipe. So am I picking you up or what?"

"Totally," I said.

I knew she was right. If I was gonna do the Jesus walk, it meant doing the small groups and prayer. I had to plug in. I needed not just to pray, but seriously to be prayed for. Plus, I missed my mom so much. Anyone who's lost a parent, a child, a best friend, a spouse knows that terrible dreadful sensation of *needing* to call that person and not being able to. It's the stuff that painting *The Scream* is made of.

I really didn't want to go to the old lady Bible study. I wanted to go to my mom's house. I wanted to sit on her couch and have her pour me giant mug of dark-roast coffee and cry and cry and say, "Joe's being so mean, Mommy." And she'd say, "Your daddy can be a piece of work, too. He'll calm down." I wanted a safe place for a week or so to cool down. I wanted support. I needed it. I felt like a soldier with his arms blown off. I couldn't fight.

But Meg was right and so I agreed to let her scoop me up, mess that I was, and dump me on the lap of the church ladies. And what those church ladies did, let me tell you was a miraculous life- not to mention marriage- saver.

My women, upon hearing my story, made a schedule. On that week-long list was the name of one sister each day that would pray and fast for me and Joseph. I was asked to fast from something each day for a week.

"You don't have to give up food," Meg said, making certain I would not attempt a weeklong hunger strike against discord in my household. "You can fast from anything. Coffee?"

"Absolutely not. I'd rather give up food than that," I said. "I get it. I'll fast from something each day. Starting with food tomorrow."

"Right. Great," she said. She seemed surprised that I understood the concept of fasting.

"Yogis often practice fasting for spiritual reasons as well," I said.

"Well," Meg's guard always rose a little when I mentioned yoga, "Jesus does say that there are certain things that will only come out by prayer *and* fasting. Plus, it can just be a super effective way to focus and hear from God."

Meg gave my number to all the ladies and their numbers to me. The plan was that each day, one woman would fast from food and pray and clamor the gates of Heaven on my behalf. Then, each evening at 7, that woman would call me and pray with me for my marriage and then tell me any impressions and insights she felt she'd gained in her prayer time and any scriptures which came to mind. Thereby we would discern what the Lord was trying to do in me and Joe and our marriage.

I felt so loved, so cared for. I even felt mothered.

It was two days into the fast, as I was sitting in my warm jammies, snuggled under a blanket by the fire which Joe had lit, that I laid my mind open and became still before the Lord. A fresh breeze blew through my mind carrying four simple words: "He needs you, Shannyn."

And with it, the impression that (1) I needed to stay and (2) That God was working out something much bigger than my marriage to Joseph. I knew then that the additional five days of fasting and praying was icing on the cake. I had my answer. I would stay because God said I had to, and crazy Christian as that sounds, it was more than good enough for me.

Wouldn't it be fun if after great big life lessons and prayer and fasting we then systematically hit a season of rest and bliss and ease? Wouldn't it just be…grand?

I think so, but it's not yet been my experience that that's how things play out. This season was no different.

Life began to happen again. Joe wasn't treating me like a china doll any more. Alex was still needing to be shuttled here there and everywhere, including weekly encounters with my ex. Liam was still not napping or sleeping through the night and Joe…was still…Joe.

My church lady friends did their level best to counsel me in the ways of parenting success, emphasizing the importance of keeping a schedule and maintaining consistency. These were pioneering women, both the young and old ones. They grew their own food. They baked their own bread. They . . . stayed at home. I couldn't compete.

But the thing they had that I wanted and needed the most was a content prayer life. I didn't want to read all those books they talked about. I had my Bible. I didn't want to scrap book. I had my yoga. I didn't want to come to the cookie exchange. I didn't eat that stuff. But I did want to pray. I did want to read that Bible and unpack it together like I used to with my Shakespeare friends.

I wanted that and got it and so overflowed with joy and hope at the power of praying in the name of Jesus that I had to share it. You ever had a bite of the best brownie in the world and your first impulse after you go, "Um, yum, nom nom nom," and taste the deep dark gooeyness of it all, is to turn to the person nearest you and say, "Omg! You have to taste this!"

It was like that with me and Jesus and the power of prayer. A friend would call to chat and mention that she and her hubby were looking at renting a store front for their business. My response? "I'd love to pray for you. Can I pray for you right now?"

A listener would call the radio station and begin to tell their sob story. "Is it OK if I pray for you?" I would say.

I prayed for everyone.

I prayed for a friend, raised in the Jewish faith, who'd lost her son to an overdose and changed her name to Shanti to begin a new life.

I prayed for some guy in the grocery store who looked like he was about to wale on his kid for tipping over a display. I ducked in and said, "Hey...I know this sounds weird, but I'm a Jesus person and I'd love to pray for you. Would that be cool?"

Time after time with only one exception, people didn't just say "Um...OK?" (read "awkward") but instead they practically shouted "YES! PLEASE PRAY FOR ME!"

We need it. It's vital. We soak it up like the desert drinks the water. We are insatiably thirsting for the living water. All of us.

The one person, by the way, who refused prayer, was a pagan health food store employee who, as she informed me in heart breaking detail, had been desperately wounded by the hypocrisy of church. I prayed for her in my head. I prayed for the thousands like her.

And another thing happened. I sent out tapes and resumes to Christian radio stations, because my new Bible said, "Do everything you do for the glory of the one who made you." I wanted to use the gifting he'd given me in radio, to give Him glory and to tell everyone I knew about this awesome Jesus who consistently gets a terrible rap.

I wanted to talk about this Savior who paid our ransom. Why should I be taking caller Number10 for tickets to see Maroon 5 when I could actually *help* somebody?

Guess what? With 15 years of radio experience, not one Christian station would talk to me, with the exception of Family Life Radio, who told me that they didn't think I was a fit for the position. So, I continued to help the next in line at Starbucks and take caller 10 at Magic and now teach yoga in Detroit and ride the wave of my family until one day, while I was at my daughter's school helping out as a playground monitor, my cell phone rang.

"Hello," I said tentatively, not recognizing the number.

"Hello, Shannyn?" It was a booming-radio sounding voice. I did not recognize it.

"Yes, this is she." I gestured to another mom that I would be right back and ducked into a quiet corner of the playground.

"Hi, Shannyn. This is Frank, general manager of Detroit's Christian F.M. 103.5 WMUZ, the Light."

Wow, I thought, what a giant intro.

"Yes. Hi Frank." I'd heard of him and of his station and it was the one place I'd not applied to, mostly because they had a mid-day host who scared me to death. I couldn't listen to his show. In fact my pastor, Jim, told me not to. Jim said, "Let's just keep the first thing first. Enjoy the honeymoon, Shannyn." Listening to the show made me feel like anyone who didn't think there were little baby dinosaurs on the ark was not a Christian. He had a huge following of loyal listeners. I couldn't imagine hanging around the water cooler with him. I did not think I could pass his *is she really a Christian* test. If the kinder, gentler Family Life Radio didn't think I was a fit there, surely I was an ugly sister trying to shoehorn my way into a glass slipper at WMUZ, but there he was...Frank...calling...me.

"How can I help you?" I said.

"Well," he said clearing his throat, "we've had a terrible loss here at the station."

"Oh, I'm so sorry to hear that."

"Our morning show co-host Rhonda Hart has died. It was very sudden."

"Oh, NO! Oh, no, that's terrible," I said.

Rhonda was a legacy Detroit jock. She'd been everywhere. Half the places I'd worked, she'd been at too, but at different times. She had a heart of gold. She came from the metal scene, mostly and was known as "Rockin' Rhonda" until one day she had an encounter with Jesus and it broke her addictions and set her free. She was a girl on fire like me...only she died. It was a great loss indeed.

"Did you know Rhonda?" Frank asked, as if he detected my connection to the news.

"No," I said, "but I respected her. I'm so sorry."

"Thank you." His tone was fatherly. "Well, obviously this leaves us with an opening and a very important one at that."

"Sure..." I said. I made eye contact with the playground mom and put up a *one more minute* finger.

"And as you know, Rhonda was a real pro and I'll need a real pro in this spot."

"Sure, of course."

"And this morning, I was asking around the coffee pot here at the station if anyone knew of any Christians who worked in Detroit radio and your name came up."

"Really? Great!" I thought...wow! The word's on the street!

"Yes, so... is it true? Are you a Christian?"

I could hear the "moment of truth" sound in my head.

"Yes. I am!" I declared. With my whole heart.

"How would you describe your position in the body of Christ?"

Wow! I thought. Holy Moly. There's a question for you. "My position in the body? I'm sorry, Frank, I really don't speak hardly any Christianese. I would consider myself a born-again evangelical Christian, if that's what you mean. I'm both those things. I'm born again. And I'm evangelical."

"Well, great!" he said with a laugh. "That's a good thing. I would love to meet you. Can we set up a time?"

Now here again, you would think that with the Lord's hand of blessing on this, that it would be a smooth transition into my new Christian morning show gig. Nothing could be further from true. I met Frank and the meeting went well. Then he proceeded to interview me eleven – count them – eleven more times, sometimes in person, sometimes on the phone, each time with a new question about my Christianity and beliefs that he'd uncovered. It was months of the inquisition...

"What do you think about other religions? Say…Hinduism? Would you call Hinduism a false religion?"

"Well," I'd say, "I think that God loves people. All people for all time and all over the planet and I think He's calling out to them and always has and will. Is it false? Well, unless it's teaching Jesus as the atonement for your sins and the resurrection of Christ our living God, then yep…I guess it's false." Much to my surprise, I cleared that hurdle.

"Abortion?" he asked the next time.

"It's wrong. I support a woman's right to be born. But I also have lots of friends who have had abortions and I still love them." Cleared that hurdle too.

"Gay marriage?" he said leaning in as if adjusting his imaginary microscope.

"My friends Paul and Tom have been together for longer than any of my other friends. I'm divorced. *Most* of our buddies are divorced. They are still together. It's been 20 years now. That said, I believe the Bible and sometimes what it says is not what I like. In that case, I am wrong and the Bible is right. This is a case like that."

This went on and on with a random phone call here and there. This was a "what do you want to be when you grow up" job, and it was just out of reach of the bills, still stacking high at the casa de Caldwell.

In that season, I'd picked up the habit of reading the Proverb of the Day...you know Proverbs 1 on the 1st, 2 on the 2nd, etc.? And I was finding it...wait for the Christianese...convicting. It was...oops... more Christianese...speaking to my brokenness.

The Proverbs were telling me to step up my game. Not to "eat the bread of idleness"...to get off the couch and back into my garden to get to canning like the church ladies did.

It was telling me to steer clear of adultery, which is such a trap for so many men and women in difficult marriages.

They were telling me that it was better for Joseph to live on the corner of a roof top than...with ME: bitter, nagging wife.

That it was better to have peace and quiet in our house with just a crust of bread than a house full of feasting with strife.

I was seeking the wrong things. I wanted to pay our bills more than I wanted peace.

I wanted to be right more that I wanted peace.

I was the problem. I wasn't the whole problem, but certainly at least half the problem was me.

And when Joseph would come home to find me reading said Proverbs, his reaction was always something like "Oh, GREAT! You're reading THAT AGAIN?" and then he'd leave with a slam of the old wooden door and go to a friend's to drink beer and play video games.

It seemed like the closer to holiness I drew, the more it repelled him. "No one wants to party with a church lady," he'd say.

Church ladies have parties of their own, I'd think, but I held my tongue and prayed. I was learning.

CHAPTER 10

ODE TO SILENCE. ODE TO JOY!

Lord, I am dizzy. Remind me that I am safe in the shelter of your wings.
Ground me in your truth. You are the rock. I cling to you now.

You know how Paul tells us to *consider it joy when we go through trials of many kinds, because in those times the Lord draws near to us?*

That was so very true there on the wreckage of my parents' house, so true in how God gave me those 3D glasses to see the kingdom draw near in the purple shrouds and found objects.

He did it again in this next season, because in that time, although Frank was dragging his heels into the rapidly setting tar, we still couldn't pay our bills. Joe was still allergic to the church lady bit. He was still yelling and screaming, although for the most part I was no longer yelling back and that made a huge difference. Still, the house was beyond stressed when, in the dead of winter, Joe's truck broke down.

Now, this was not a *get around* truck. It was a working truck. Tree-trimmer, mason Joseph needed a truck to do his still-too-hard-to-find work. Any hope of Joe working ground to a halt in the center of our back yard. A giant bright red heap of a money pit, rather than money maker, sat in the snow, hood up.

Joe delivered the news like a doctor in a waiting room. "It's gonna take $350 to fix it."

"We only HAVE $350," I said and told him to look for a cheaper fix.

"I SAID it's gonna take $350." His Marine Corp bark was back.

"OK," I said and slunk to my room with my Bible and closed the door and lay on the bed and hugged tight to its soft black leather binding and cried into the gold on its edges. In my heart I cried out to the Lord because I did not have one single dollar to feed my family. Not one buck to go the dollar store and get some noodles. We were broke. Along with most of our foreclosed- on neighbors, we were tipping on the edge of the cliff of the bankrupting Detroit.

Then the tender voice of our loving Father spoke to me again. "I know your heart, little mother."

I felt so known and understood because I didn't want the food for me. I could fast. I wanted the food for them. For my kids, and I thought, how could this be? I've got an education. I've got experience. We live a simple life. Why can't I feed my kids? Why can't my husband?

And just then, the Lord gave me a picture of a giant bowl full of flour. There was a pit in the center of the flour and then I saw an egg crack over the bowl and land in the pit. Then a spoon full of water poured in and began to stir. This, I thought, is how the old women in the U.P. used to make homemade pasta growing up! I remembered it now.

I went to the kitchen. Checking in my fridge, I found one egg, flour, a little bit of butter and the bottom of a shaker of parmesan. I followed the recipe the Lord provided and made homemade noodles for dinner that night. The kids still swear it's the best meal I've ever made and they do not know that we were broke the day I first made it.

Also in that time, Noreen (remember the greeter from the first day of church) called and informed me that the Lord told her to pay my phone bill, and a friend of Rebecca's pulled into my driveway and handed me a check for … $350. I never told anyone, until now, about how much the fix on the truck had cost. The Lord provides, I thought, and it seems that He often uses His people to do it.

I was at Reba's house and having a peppermint tea when Frank called with a random "pop-up" interview. "Oh, no! It's Frank!" I said. "Should I pick it up?"

"Yes!" Reba insisted with a wave. "Take it in my bedroom."

"Hello, Frank," I said, trying not to sound like I was saying, "Hello….Newman…"

"Hi, Shannyn. I know we've done this again and again, but…"

"Yes, we certainly have, Frank," I said.

"Well, it's very important that I get this right. You understand."

"I do. I also understand that being interviewed by you is not my part time job. I've been a totally open book for you, Frank. I'm not trying to hide anything from you. What do you need to know?"

"I guess I just want to make sure that you are in line with our thinking."

He said it with a slight hesitation, as if he were speaking in code. I was sick of the hunting and pecking for my hidden subversive agenda.

There was not one and I was beginning to resent the suggestion that there was. "Frank, I am what I am. I am a Jesus-loving, sold-out follower. I've lost most of my friends to it. My marriage is a wreck and following the Bible is my only hope. I have a great church family. I go to Bible study. My kids are my world. I practice yoga and it makes me feel closer to God…yes *that* God. The God. If that is not a fit, then lose my number, Frank. I'm not your girl."

Long silence. I was the first to break it.

"And if I am your girl, put it in writing, because you're not the only dog in the hunt and I'm looking for a full time job."

"Well, are you close to a job anywhere else?" He was almost mocking and I refused to accept that any longer. He may have been *a* boss, but he was not *my* boss...not yet.

"Very. Next time you call me, let it be to tell me my contract is ready or you are done. OK? I don't mean it ugly, Frank, but enough is enough."

"OK..." He sounded like he was backing slowly away. "I understand..." And then in a salesman's tone he added, "I'll be in touch!"

And he was. Frank called two days later to invite me to come and look over my contract and next thing you knew, I was working with dinosaur guy – who actually turned out to be a really nice guy – and Frank was one of the best bosses I'd ever had.

My first order of business was to make the biggest, most joyful splash I possibly could. So my listeners and I created something called the *Joy Flash Mobs*. We'd meet at a church basement and learn a dance to a rockin' gospel song called "Joy" by Niyoki. Google it. You'll love it. We'd practice the dance again and again and then on a day and time that only my very small audience knew, we'd mix ourselves into giant crowds and erupt into praise dancing, just to disappear back into the crowd when the song was done. We did the Tigers home opener, Motown Winter Blast and a bunch more. Tons of people woke up to what the Jesus thing is all about. Or they simply felt the presence of the Lord.

One time, at a giant indoor flea market, a practicing Buddhist got caught up in the joy of it all, jumped into the middle of the mob and then accepted Christ with two flash mobsters in the bathroom. Another time – and I wasn't witness to this but I was told – a number of people grabbed other flashmobsters and said, "What WAS that?" and received Christ on the spot.

The flash mobs were effective. They were contagious and (Christianese alert) the Enemy hated them. One day, our choreographer, Lizbeth's windows were bashed in on her car. Once there was a huge accident on the freeway that led to our event, closing the road. We all made it anyway and 5 people embraced the Gospel that day, 2 Muslims and 3 Hindus.

But for me, the biggest bang of all came right before the very first practice of the Joy Flash Mobs. On that day, I was doing the mommy-multi task of spooning out the dinner to plates while talking on the phone, lining up last minute details with the choreographer and Flash Mob Bob, the sound guy.

Joe began to rage.

This time the kids were there, sitting at the table for our family dinner, a tradition which I maintained from my childhood and thought of as sacred, even if I was getting off the phone real quick before we ate.

Joe hated that. To him, dinner was silent. It was not time for talking, a belief he gleaned from spending time sharing meals with brothers at a monastery he would escape to from his crazy childhood home. He could and would run to it when things were bad and they always welcomed him and his brothers.

Joe was in anything but his brotherly peace as he picked up the plate of spaghetti and salad and whipped it into the wall like a Frisbee. The plate shattered and red pasta went everywhere from ceiling to floor.

"I have to go," I said to Bob and hung up. Apparently the dollars spent on therapy for us could have been better spent, because this... well, it was not going to work.

Alex's eyes were giant and scared. Liam looked like he was in shock. He was bigger now. Not a baby. He understood.

Alex took Liam by the hand. "Come on, baby" she said, "Let's go to my room for a little bit."

When they were gone, I said to Joe, "That's it. It's over."

"*I'll* say when it's over, Lady." Joe was actually growling at me.

But I'd turned a mental corner. I'd gotten freer, stronger and wiser in the faith. I knew that the Bible said not to divorce Joseph, but it did not say that I had to live with him while we were married. That's a point which Reba had made to me the day she told me where she hid her house key, the day I'd packed my escape box with couple of days' worth of toiletries and changes of clothes for me and the kids

"When you rage at me, Joe," I'd told him calmly days later when things were calm, "should that ever happen again, here's what I'm going to do. I'm going to take the kids and we are going to get in the car and go away. We are going to leave."

It had been warm and sunny the day I told him that, and as we drank black coffee on our back deck, neither of us thought that day would come again. "Now understand, sweet heart," I'd told him, "that if we do leave, it does not mean we are leaving you. We are leaving the situation, OK? Cuz the kids are getting too big and as their mom, I cannot let them learn that this is how families run. How husbands and wives act. How moms and dads are. I don't mean we are leaving *you*. It means we are leaving the situation, OK?"

And so, with the seed already planted, and the next time something went flying (in this case it was a lamp), I calmly said, "Come on kids, let's go!"

Joseph was silent. He just watched quietly as I grabbed my purse and led the kids out the side door. We drove around until I could see he'd left the house and then I pulled in behind Rebecca's place.

I shut off the car, unbuckled and turned in my seat to see my precious babies. I'd wanted so much more for them than this. I looked at little Alex, now 12 years old, on the brink of her own big girl choices. My heart broke at everything she'd been through: losing her grandparents, her daddy leaving, the mess that was me and Joseph. And Liam, only three. He didn't ask to come into this mess. I brought him. We brought him. It was *our* fault.

"Listen, you guys." I tried making my voice as calm and steady as possible. "We are going to be OK. Everything is going to be OK. Every single last thing is going to be OK."

I looked straight into their giant blue eyes, the eyes they each got from their daddies. "God is going to do a miracle, because we need a miracle. He will. He promises, not me."

They looked like they were listening to a French dub on their favorite movie. They knew it, but they couldn't understand it.

"Now, I don't know what that miracle will *be*," I said, "but I know it is coming. Maybe God will do a miracle and fix everything broken with Mommy and Daddy."

"Yeah, and maybe Daddy won't leave," said my hopeful three-year-old from the back seat.

"Well, sweetheart, Daddy didn't leave. We left, but just for a sleepover at Miss Rebecca's until Mommy and Daddy are better at talking to each other."

"Yeah," Alex said. With big girl sarcasm.

"And maybe God will do a miracle and sustain you and you!" I tried to smile as I bopped them each on the nose with the tip of my pointer. "Either way, it's going to be fine. It's gonna be great. Promise. Let's go."

And we popped out of the car, grabbed our escape box and went to find the hidden key.

It was the next morning, wearing the same clothing we left in, that we had the first Joy Flash Mob practice. I could barely act like anything was OK for myself, let alone my kids, let alone the 200-some listeners who'd gathered in a church yard that morning to learn a dance of joy.

But my acting degree proved handy again and we all learned the routine. After everyone got in their cars and minivans to drive home, the kids and I went to dinner with church friends, and I spilled my beans.

"I thought something was wrong," my girlfriend Lori said, stirring raw sugar cubes into her iced tea. I personally couldn't drink. Or eat. "You didn't seem yourself at the practice."

"Oh no. I tried so hard to come off cool."

"You were fine!" she said. She sounded like a mom who tells you your awful school picture is cute, "It's only cuz we know you. Have you talked to Jim about this?"

Ya gotta love a friend whose first question is, "Have you talked to pastor?"

Ya gotta love a pastor who makes that question a reasonable one to ask.

"Not yet," I said, "It just happened last night and then this morning, well...Joy Flash Mob practice and then...well... here we are!"

"You should let him know. He should know this is going on. He'd want to. So he can pray for you, if nothing else." She'd made her dinner choice and folded up the menu, setting it aside.

"I know, but girl, I am just so sick of needing help. I'm so sick and tired of being that girl. I want to be the girl who helps, not the one who *needs* help."

I opened a box a crayons for Liam to color his placemat.

"Ya, but today is not that day." Lori shook her head kindly at me, lightening the mood. "Someday will be that day, but girl, today you are the one who needs help. So let us help you!"

"You're absolutely right," I agreed. "It's true. It sucks and you're right."

Just like that.

And so in the car on the way home, I called Jim, who agreed to come over to talk. He said he would call Joe to arrange the meet at our house that night. I was hopeful, skeptical and a little fearful, too. But God was becoming more and more my strong tower and I knew whatever came my way, I could run to him and be safe.

Jim brought a "heavy" named Jack Mrrish with him as he showed up to triage the Caldwell's *again*. I was surprised to see Mike there with Jim because Jack was a cop. I didn't know we were so bad that the police had to come and that's exactly what Joseph's opening line was as we pulled out our wooden chairs to take a seat at the peace talks . . . or maybe the settlement of land agreement.

Jim seemed to sense Joseph's dismay with the tag team of pastor and bouncer. "Don't worry, Joe. I'm not saying anyone's a bad guy here. Sometimes it's just good to have more than one voice. The Apostles worked in twos, after all."

I was afraid Joseph might put his war paint on and let it fly, but he just said tightly, "Good answer."

I gave Jim a "see what I have to put up with" glance.

"Well, you guys are the ones who called me," Jim said.

"She did," Joe said.

"And you picked the time. Let's not play games, OK? If you guys are gonna work this out, we are going to have to stay focused."

"OK," I said, and prayed silently, Oh God, please, please let peace come of this.

"Yes." Joe said it like the man's vote carried double weight.

Jim pulled out a leather bound journal and pen and said, "So, what's been going on?"

Joe and I both started in on our sides of the story at the same time, our voices stacking like plates in the window of a busy restaurant, waiting to be delivered to their proper place.

"OK. One at a time." Jim tapped his ball point on his binding as if it were a judge's gavel. "Joe, you go first, and while he's talking, Shannyn . . . you stay silent. Then it will be your turn."

Dear God, I thought, when will we ever learn this very basic skill?

"Cool," I said. "And when it's my turn . . . Joe has to be quiet?"

"Yes," Jim said, with an appeasing laugh. "OK, Joe. What's going on? Go!"

Joe unpacked the fact that I was selfish and materialistic and a diva and a terrible housekeeper.

I, by the grace of God, kept silent until he was finished. For my part, I shared the lack of work, the raging, yelling, throwing things. How the kids were learning it and how I, as their mom, couldn't allow it to go on.

When I was through, Jim took off his John Lennon glasses and rubbed between his eyes. "Do you guys want it to work? I mean, do you want to work it out? Joe?"

To my amazement, Joe said, "Yes. Yes I do, Jim."

Jim turned to me. "Shannyn?"

My answer was different. "Um . . . I guess? But I'm tired, Jim. I'm at my end. I'm pretty done, man." I searched his eyes for recognition.

"I understand. Let me ask this: Are you willing to *try* to work it out?"

Good question, I thought. Could this be the final exit off the highway to hell we'd been driving on? And if so, would *God* want me to take it? With an almost defeated sigh I said, "Sure."

"OK. GOOD! That's good you guys!" Jim said, clapping his hands and rubbing them together. He sounded like a soccer coach. "Next question: Do you give me authority in this situation? Will you do, or at least try to do, what I say?"

"Yes." My answer was immediate. He was my pastor, after all. Not really Joe's. Joe just visited my church from time to time.

"Joe?"

"Yes, Jim. I do." Joe spoke as if a 5-star general just boarded ship. I was floored. I had never seen Joseph hand over his authority. Never.

"OK you guys. There are a couple of different ways you can approach this." Jim was into game plan time for the team. I expected him to draw Joe and me with X's and O's on a field shaped like our house.

"I'm gonna lay the ways out for you and then you two can pick which one you feel will work best, OK?"

We nodded.

"Obviously, you need some room to breathe. Some time to let this air out. So one choice would be that Joseph stays here with the kids and Shannyn you move out for a week or some other predetermined length of time and visit the kids on set days."

"Nope," I said. "Not that one."

"OK. Another choice: Shannyn, you to stay with the kids while Joe goes away for some set time and has visits with the kids."

I couldn't believe we were coming to this.

"The third option is probably the hardest, but if you think you can do it, it's what I would actually recommend and it's this: you guys both stay in the same house with the kids. Before I leave here, we put together a calendar of every single thing you'd need to talk about for say…a week. Tomorrow's Sunday, so say it's from Sunday to Sunday. We pick Joe's days and times to go out and do whatever he wants. He doesn't have to even tell you what he's doing. And we pick which days and times Shannyn goes out and Joe…same thing…it's her time. We write down everything, which is picking up which kid and when. And then you guys practice the spiritual discipline of fasting for that week, but you're not fasting from food. You're fasting from speech, OK? Not a word. Not one word. Nothing. Not even a grunt. Don't even make noises at one another. And then we meet at my office after church next Sunday and see how it went and what there is to talk about. How does that sound?"

He looked like he just made a pitch for a billion dollar movie.

"Sounds great!" I said. "If he can't talk, he can't yell."

"It's you, too…now," Jim said raising his Spock-like eyebrow. "Joe?"

"Let's do it," Joe said.

Once again, I was flabbergasted – and even more so when we put every detail down on paper and posted in on the fridge. And thus began the first peaceful, quiet week of our young married life.

Not talking to each other proved an excellent fit for me and my true love. I, it probably comes as no surprise, talk . . . a lot. Probably too much. Yep. It's a gift.

And Joe? Every word he said sounded like a fight to me. It was good to go back to the initial advice the Lord had given me. To be still. Very still. Even the tongue. Still.

Our test drive of said silence was at Yates Cider Mill for the first ever Joy Flash Mob!

Sunday after church we drove without a sound to the mill. Joseph tried to talk once in the car.

"Thát's the woods," he said pointing out the window to the left, "That's our woods. It's where we had our first date. Paint Creek, it's right down there."

I shook my head. I would not talk. Not a word.

I met with the flashmobsters and we all mixed ourselves into the busy, cinnamon doughnut smelling crowd. At 2:30 on the dot, with Joseph watching from a distance, Liam on his shoulders, Flash Mob Bob dropped a needle on the record and the first Joy Flash Mob took flight.

"What are they doing?" a wide-eyed man asked in amazement.

"I think they're dancing!" said a cheerleader-looking girl to his right.

And we were! I was, too. With all my heart I joined my hands with my brothers and sisters in Christ in a circle going round and round and in and out as we sang at the top of our lungs and danced like David before the Lord.

"This joy that I have, the world didn't give it to me!" the lyric goes, "This joy that I have, the world can't take it away."

And that was *true*. I sang, we all did, from the top of my lungs. It was awesome. A 6-foot-tall woman in the front row messed up big time and that made it even *better*! For real. Google it. Youtube it: First Joy Flash Mob. You'll see.

Round and round we went, hootin' and hollerin' "YES, LORD!" and "JESUS!" We ended *Hava Nagila* style, all joining hands above our heads and dancing toward the center. With a pause we turned and shouted the final line of the song which says, "Jesus is the best thing. He makes my heart sing." And seamlessly mixed back into the crowd and vanished.

And it was true. It didn't matter so much what happened with me and Joseph. I'd make the most biblical choices I could make, but on that day, I had the perfect husband. His name was Jesus and He was all I needed to have joy.

That week was a treasure.

I could take walks with my friend without having to ask Joseph's permission.

I recognized that I did talk too much. I wasted a ton of words. If oil were my words, this world would run on solar by now. I would have exhausted our resources.

The Lord gave me a dream that week. It was a water dream and in it, Joseph and I were floating down a lazy river, a manmade one. It was indoors and underground. It twisted and turned in the darkish caverns and we slid easily from stop to stop where we'd rest or just splash around. We didn't talk. We were friends. That's it. And I remember thinking, what do water dreams mean? Maybe in this case it was being born again, because next Sunday, after church, Joseph and I met with Jim and Jack in his office to see how it went. We squeezed into the tiny, book-filled space, shuffling around our folding chairs to make them all fit. In that leading way, Jim, said, "So...how's it been?"

"Good!" Joe said.

"Great!" I said. "Awesome!"

Joe looked, well, humble. "I have something I wrote and if it's OK with you, I'd just like to read it."

Jim nodded.

Here is what he wrote:

Dear Shannyn,

I've failed you. I'm sorry. Please forgive me. I've been a terrible husband to you.

The only reason I can figure out for that is that I'm broken, because I've really tried.

The only solution to my brokenness that I can figure out is Jesus and making Him the center of my life and our marriage. To that end, here is what I propose.

I accept Jesus and get baptized immediately.
We begin premarital counseling with Jim and Megan.
You re-marry the new creation.

Should you accept my proposal, here is what my vows will be.

I will love and cherish you above myself, esteeming your needs greater than mine.
I will never raise my voice to you in anger again.
I will pray with you and for you daily.
If we come on problems, I will immediately seek Godly help so our love will never fail.

Please, give me that chance to be the man, husband and father that God is calling me to be.
I will always love you, Shannyn and I pray you will go with me on this new journey.

When he was finished reading, Joseph folded the handwritten document, tucked it in his coat pocket and bowed his head.

"I think something holy is happening here," Jim said. He got down on his knees. "I think we should pray."

Jack tucked his Tigers cap under his elbow as Joe took to his knees and wept.

Jim prayed. "Lord, we just acknowledge your presence here. We want to praise you, Jesus. Joe, would you like to repeat the sinner's prayer with me?"

"Yes, Jim." Joe was red-faced and in tears. "Yes, I would."

I was dumbfounded. What was happening was unbelievable but real. What would my life be like now, I wondered, with a saved husband?

"Lord, Jesus. I am broken," Jim said, and Joseph repeated through his tears. "I'm a sinful man. I can't do it without you. I can't do it without you."

"Come into my heart, Lord," Joe repeated with quiet reverence. "I give myself to you."

The Spirit of God was so rich in the place, I expected the walls to shake and send the books flying, but there was a perfect stillness. Jim led on, "Thank you for saving me. In Jesus' name."

Joseph repeated the words with the preciousness that comes from deep understanding. It was not a magic wand, the name of Jesus. It was truly a life line.

We all said, "Amen," with a sigh of fullness.

Joseph David Caldwell did exactly what he'd proposed he'd do and was baptized in a baby pool after church the next Sunday right on Main Street in Downtown Royal Oak.

Our family, our brothers and sisters, were all there. It was a victory for all of us. For the sisters who'd prayed for and with me. For the girl who dropped off the money. For Jim, for Meg, for my brother, who'd been praying forever and for the Kingdom of God.

"Angels are rejoicing," Meg whispered in my ear as Jim in his khakis and t-shirt led Joe in his swim trunks and t-shirt though the Apostle's Creed and then plunged him into the icy cold water in the noonday October sun.

"Remember this, my friend." Meg hugged me close to her collar, her breath warming my neck from the chill of the wind. "And when you can't remember, I'll be here to remind you."

God is God. The victory was won.

And yet, the battle in me . . . it continued to rage.

When people say "we become a new man in Christ," it's true, but it's not always instant.

As Noreen said one day, "Sometimes God works like the ocean. We are sitting on the beach watching the tide go in and out. We think the coastline isn't changing. God, he's working under water where we can't see, but He is making some big changes."

It's true. Sometimes, like a tornado, Christ carries our broken-away, throwing-up sickness and depravity as far as the east is from the west in one blinding flash of terrible glory. And sometimes it's just a lazy river that chips away at our old way of thinking and being. But that change comes. He's an unstoppable force.

We were learning and improving. I held my tongue and prayed and switched to forgiveness when we stumbled because I knew that I did not war against flesh and blood, but against spiritual forces in heavenly places. This battle was not mine. I didn't win Joseph to Jesus. Jesus wooed Joseph to himself through loving kindness, not condemnation and it's that same kindness that the Bible says draws us to repentance. I know how crazy Christian it sounds, but Jesus Himself said to *bless* those who curse you, so and I believed Him for my life.

So I prayed hard in the Spirit and fasted.

I was teaching myself to esteem Joseph higher than myself. To remember to burn into my thick skull that love is patient, kind, does not envy, doesn't boast; is not arrogant or rude... you kidding me?

I had the world's shortest fuse and I resented Joe, John, Mom, Dad . . . the list went on and on. Love does not rejoice in wrong doing, but in truth. Love bears all, hopes all things, and endures *all* things. But look at the end!

1 Corinthians 13:8 says Love *never* fails.

It was a promise. And I knew God never broke His promises. Therefore, if I could manage to endure and believe and bear and hope and submit, He had a fool-proof plan.

All the while we were doing our "pre-marital counseling" with Jim and Meghan, and trying to live what we guessed was a "normal Christian life" and "fellowship" (Christianese for hanging out with your friends). One evening in March, our fellowship night was clothing swap with my church lady friends at the home of the (Christianese alert, again) worship leader, Laurel Merz.

Laurel was and is a total boss. She's tall and bold and dresses like it's the 80's. She's a hipster to the max and she sings like a born again Aretha Franklin, unless Aretha, that is, is born again, and then she just sings like Aretha. She's got soul. Deep, deep down.

The party was at her house and a ton of us came with bags and bags of clothing and shoes and jewelry to trade. We had a blast that night –

Playing dress up and noshing on olives and feta and grapes.

Trying on scarves like movie stars and laughing our heads off while sipping goblets of pomegranate juice.

Trying on hats and blazers and even some blue jeans. We all found a zillion treasures.

I was decked out in my new earrings and paper boy hat as I packed my bag up with the rest of the gals to go home from the evening's hunt. Laurel gave me a warm hostess hug goodnight.

"It was such a blast!" I said. "Thank so much for having me!"

"Oh my goodness, girl! Thank you for coming! We all totally scored!" She twinkled and pointed at her lovely new pineapple bracelet. "I can't wait for my mom to go to bed so my hubs and I can kick back," she whispered her chocolate-infused breath in my ear. "That's the downside of your mom living with you. You can never be alone."

She winked and laughed as she give me an "out ya go" tap on the back. Now if this all sounds a bit familiar, it should. Because it was this exact evening and this exactly exchange that tipped my scale and sent me back to Jim and Meg's house the evening he would propose the healing season.

With her obviously well-meaning remark about her mom, the entire wonderful evening circled the drain and ran out. I burst into a flood of tears. "You should be thankful," I said…"at least you HAVE your mom. I have no one."

I was the unraveling drunk girl at the end of a party…only… I was not drunk. I was broken. Still shattered. Saved. Born Again. Evangelical. Scripture quoting, Kingdom-minded Christian morning show host, and yet broken, it seemed, beyond repair. The look on Laurel's face showed her embarrassment and shock for me. It was like I'd just opened my trench coat and flashed her.

"I'm so sorry. I'm so embarrassed," I said, "I'm good. I'm just sad. I can drive."

I tried to gather myself.

"It's OK, honey. I know. You're right," Laurel said, but she looked as taken back as me. Her husband . . . he looked like he regretted resurfacing from his man cave so soon.

But we hugged and God-blessed right on out the door and I sat in my car and wept and wept and wept.

April was around the corner. The season. The anniversary of the tornado breathing down my neck. The snow melting. The smell of dirt and grass. The Easter decorations already out at the neighbors'. The eggs, bringing me back to that Easter dinner with my folks at my house, when I lied to my dad about his Don McClean record and watched them drive away for the last time.

It was too much. I was still breaking and I had asked the Lord a thousand million times to take away the pain and still here I sat, hunched over my steering wheel and crying off my girl-party make-up.

"PLEASE! PLEASE! PLEASE!" I cried at the top of my lungs to the Lord "Take away the pain. Take it AWAY!"

I could barely feel my hands on the wheel to drive home. It felt like all of me was blown away. I'd asked Him to heal me and He had chosen in His wisdom to leave me broken. I guess, I thought, that's how you need me, then. So...broken it is.

Now people will say, myself included, that "broken is beautiful" and to an extent, I agree. It can be, and is, but I believe in a restoring, healing God who came to reconcile *everything*. My hope is set on Him...His way of life. I wanted healing. I'd read my Bible. I knew He could do it.

I also knew that, for whatever reason, He was not doing it. I was still a wreck. But I was a mess who was standing on His word and His word told me in Psalm 147:3 that He heals the brokenhearted and binds up their wounds. I *was* the brokenhearted. Why wasn't He healing me?

But His word told me, too, in Hebrews 11:1 that faith was being sure of what I hoped for and certain of what I did not see. And I hoped to live a happy, healthy, healed life with a loving husband and children secure in their home and comfy in their own skin. My God told me He was the God of ALL hope, not some...not sometimes... all hope. *All*.

As I drove, my heart joined the psalmist's cry in Psalm 27:13-14 "I *believe* I shall look upon the goodness of the Lord in the land of the living! Wait for the Lord; be strong. Let your hearts take courage; wait for the Lord!"

But GOD! My deep called out to His: "How LONG? How LONG must I wait?"

The red light that blurred through my tears kept me from moving on and His gentle presence reminded me of His first admonition, back in my bedroom. Back at my breakdown-breakthrough *Be still and Know that I am God* moment. Tender peace in His silent answer filled me up as the light turned a spring-like green. It was time to go. It was time to let go. But how?

CHAPTER 11

THE FREE-AT-LAST
DITCH EFFORT

*Lord, thank you for the way that you heal. Thank you for my prayer
partners. I pray that you will fill them over-full so in their generous outpour-
ing, they come away encouraged and refreshed. We are yours, Jesus. Your will
be done.*

The next day was our pre-marital counseling again. Meg had
made good strong coffee and poured it into giant clay mugs she
and Jim had brought back from a mission to Ethiopia.

"Dude," she said, in the deepest, most profound way, "You guys
must try Ethiopian coffee sometime. It's unbelievable."

"I *know*!" I agreed, eyes wide at the thought. "You guys are killing
me, between you and Reba I can't stop hearing about it. I want to
try it!"

"We'll do it someday," she shouted back as she walked to the
kitchen to get, I was sure, something sweet.

I was right. She came back with "just plain store bought cookies."
She refused to take credit. It was Aldi's.

Joe scooped up two chocolate chippers and ate the first in one bite.

"Dude!" I said. "Easy, killer!"

"That's impressive," Jim said, pulling himself up to his seat. "So, how's things, ya crazy kids?"

"Good." Joe sipped from his mug. "It's been good. Nothing really to report."

What a joy it was to have "nothing to report." No drama. No new wounds. Not even a mountaintop. The middle road would do just fine, I thought.

"Shannyn…" Jim said. He was now used to having to orchestrate civil conversation between us.

"Well…good…I guess. Pretty good." I shifted in my chair, trying to decide if I wanted to open the can of worms that was the ladies' clothing swap and my meltdown.

"Really?" Meg give me a "let's get real here" glance.

Sure that one of the church ladies had called and spilled the beans about my outburst, I snapped, "Why? What did you hear?"

Meg laughed out loud. "What do you mean? You crack me up." She slid a tray of coffee, mugs and whipped cream onto the candlelit table.

But though she was laughing, I knew she could tell by looking at me that something actually had transpired. "What?" she said. She was like an 8th grader prying out a boyfriend secret. "What?"

"Did you hear about Laurel's party last night?" I said sheepishly.

"Yeah, I'm so bummed I had to miss it. Jim was out and I just couldn't get a sitter." She poured her coffee and topped it with a mound of whipped cream. Licking a dollop from her finger she said, "Was it the best?"

"It totally was. It was the best. It was a blast. We all got great stuff." I looked down into the black hole in my cup and wished I could fall in. "It was great until I lost it."

"What? What do you mean?" Her obvious alarm sounded half-joking, like there was not a chance I'd actually lost it, lost it.

"I mean, at the end when everyone was leaving Laurel said something about wishing her mom and I said she was lucky to have a mom and then I totally lost it, dude. It was a train wreck. I can't believe it."

Once I said it, it was like I'd fallen off my bike. It was like that free ride down the hill on roller skates with Beth Herzog back in the day, only this time when I crash-landed on the knee with my Africa Scar, Meg was there to wash it off and kiss it.

"Oh, I'm so sorry, Shannyn!"

"What do you mean!?" I said, scooping my jaw back up from hitting the table. Being compassionate about bad things happening to me...that's one kind of grace, but compassion for me being an idiot... that's a whole new level of grace. "I'm so sorry, *Laurel!* You should have seen her. She was like what in the *world* is going on?"

I tried to laugh with Meg. It was absurd.

"Give me one of those cookies," I said.

Jim, who had been listening silently, slid the plate my way and I ate one in just one bite.

"I still cry all the time. I still cry." I said, cookie crumbs flying everywhere. "And we've prayed and prayed. You know we have, but I am still...I'm still a mess."

I pushed my cup aside and lay my forehead down on the dining room table, hanging my head like a puppy who'd eaten the whole *plate* of cookies and knew I had done wrong.

"Oh, honey." Meg slid over and gently rubbed my back up and down.

"Joe, how does this affect you?" Jim said. "I mean, it must affect you, right? No man lives in a bubble."

"Yeah...it affects me." It was the only thing Joe had spoken since his first cookie. He was using his "do we really have to talk about our feelings" voice.

"Like, how?" Jim was pushing. "Do you know?"

Joe entertained another cookie and chose a sip of his coffee instead. I hope he passes on this one, I thought. It was so embarrassing.

I felt helpless. I could not fix me so dissecting my disaster seemed pointless.

"Well, you know, we're men. We want to fix things. I want to fix it...and I can't."

"Did you know that, Shannyn? That Joe feels like he should fix it...you?"

Without even lifting my head from its place I came out swinging. "Just because I'm broken doesn't mean I need fixing."

"No, no!" Jim pushed the plate of cookies out of all of our reach "You don't need to be defensive. I just didn't know if you knew. That's all."

I could feel him and Meg shooting silent glances.

Man! I thought. *Here I go again! It's amazing they let me in public!*

I lifted my gaze to look into Joseph's eyes. "I know," I said. "You don't have to fix me, baby. It's OK with me if I stay broken."

"Is that OK with YOU, Joe?" Jim asked leaning back in his chair like Freud or something. Oh BOY, I thought, *why* are we back in Shannyn's broken land? I thought this was pre-marital counseling!

"Sure, I guess." Joe said.

Jim was obviously dissatisfied with our answers. But, probably because he had a full working knowledge of the gospel of grace, he asked another question.

"Shannyn, may I ask what you mean when you say that you are . . . broken. Is it just the crying, or is there something else . . . something say, foundational?"

"I feel like I'm the walking wounded, Jim," I said. "I always have an empty spot. Sometimes it's small as my fist, sometimes it's big as a cannon ball, sometimes I can barely walk, but it's always there."

"Always? Every day?"

"Yep. On a great day, it's the size of a marble, but it's never gone. That's my broken." Joe and Jim exchanged brotherly glances. Now it was Joseph's turn to play the "See what I have to put up with" card on me.

"You know that song we sing in worship?" I sang, "*you are so good to me, you heal my broken heart, you are my Father in Heaven?*"

"Yeah. Sure." Jim nodded, his long blonde bangs in his face. "We sang it Sunday."

"Yeah, well I don't sing that song, cuz it's a lie. To me it is. *I sing you are so good to me...mmmmmmmmmmm......you are my Father in heaven.* He is so good to me. He is my Father in Heaven, but he does *not* heal my broken heart . . . obviously, and so I have to be OK with that."

"But do you hear what Joe's saying? That it's hurting *him*?"

It was like the world stopped and Jim's voice echoed like a boat going into a tunnel. *'It's not about you,'* I heard in slow mo. My hurting was hurting Joe and it needed to end somehow.

But how?

"What helps?" Jim said. It was like he was on a hunt and had picked up a scent on the trail. "Anything? Anything help at all?"

"Prayer," I said, stating the obvious.

"OK . . ." he said. "What else? Anything else help at all? You're a writer, right?"

I grasped at straws. "Yes, writing helps."

"OK, prayer helps and writing helps. Anything else?" I imagined him putting together a thousand-piece puzzle.

"Yoga, focusing on my breath."

"OK . . ." He was still diagnosing. Like *House* only healthy or those car guys who tell you to give it some gas as they listen for a sign. "And how often do the crying spells come on?"

"Like once a week, at least. That's improved. It used to be daily. It used to be all day. Progress, right?" I tried to laugh.

Jim gave me an encouraging smile. "Yes. So . . . do you know what triggered you last night? Did something happen? Was it just the last straw at Laurel's?"

"Kinda," I said. "I mean, I guess, but it wasn't just that. It's the season, Jim. It's the spring time and the snow..." I started to cry. "SEE?" I said, fanning my eyes, "The snow is melting and everyone is so excited for spring and I wish I could hide."

Meg handed me Kleenex and I dabbed my eyes.

"I wish I could hide in the basement till it's over."

"Till Spring is over? Does it get better then?" Jim sounded like he was onto something.

"Yes. Yes, it gets better on…" I paused to take a few deep breaths so I could spit out the rest of my thought. "It gets better on Mother's Day. When it's over."

I breathed deep again and found my spirit calming.

"OK, so . . . you've got some tools. Writing, breathing, praying."

"Yes," I said. "Yes."

"And you've got this hardest season, which isn't uncommon. People experience seasonal depression all the time. Usually it's the winter, but still . . ." Jim shrugged. "It's seasonal for the most part?"

"Yep. It gets worse in the spring for sure. As soon as the snow begins to melt."

Jim looked to Joe for his confirmation and Joe gave him a nod of agreement.

"Mother's Day is a hell house," Joe added, taking a big gulp of my room temp java, "and then it gets easy again. Then . . . it turns . . . summer."

"OK, so, I understand." Jim drummed the table with his fingers. "So, you're OK with living like this. But I'm not convinced that that's God's *best* for you. It seems to be affecting your husband, and thereby your household, I'm guessing."

I looked at Joseph's deep blue eyes and remembered the man I fell in love with. How could I willingly walk him through my daily torture chamber? I thought the trap was just for me.

"Do you want to try an idea on for size?" Jim said.

Suddenly I realized that I'd turned into a tornado myself, laying waste to the people I loved the most. I was twisting on an axis of my hurt and my hope.

But what was he going to pitch at me and how in the world would I ever be able to catch a pitch so strong it would or could heal my messed up garbage dump of a mind?

Jim opened the calendar on his phone. "Here's a thought," he said. "It's about 40 days until Mother's Day. Interesting number, I think."

"Now, Shannyn you go to house group on Wednesdays at Reba's right?"

"Yep."

"I'm sure she would be happy to pray with you each week."

"And if not Rebecca then someone surely will," Megan added with a nod.

Jim continued to unpack the plan. "And you go to church each Sunday, and we have prayer partners every Sunday so you can get prayer then. It doesn't matter who from, but get prayer every week, OK?"

"Yes. Sure. For sure. I'll do it."

This sounded like a feast. I'd long since gotten over my fear of being the crying girl and the girl who always needed prayer.

"So prayer on Wednesdays, prayer on Sundays and breathe and write every day, OK? Write about your pain."

Oh my heavens, I thought. I am *so* sick of talking about and writing about my pain. Enough, I thought.

But apparently it wasn't enough, not when my dearest loved ones were collateral damage.

I hesitated as I turned to Joe. I knew that a commitment to write daily would take time away from watching the kids with both eyes for an undisclosed amount of minutes. "Do I have your support in that?" I asked, "The going away to write every day part?"

"Yeah. Yes. For sure. Write, girl. Write it up!"

He rubbed my shoulders like Rocky's coach when he's gotten the tar beat out of him. Wow. As I felt the heavy weight of his strong hands supporting me, I thought, this man really does love me. That is sacrificial. He was esteeming my need greater than his own. He loved me...biblically. He was doing what he said he would when he handed me that letter.

Cherish this, Shannyn, I told myself. Do not forget.

Jim wasn't finished digging for answers. His voice was urgent. "Now," he said, eyes closed. And then he was silent. He must have been in prayer, or maybe more listening for the Lord than asking of Him. He rocked a little forward and back in his chair. "Now, do you know when it's coming on – one of these 'episodes' we can call them for lack of a better term?"

I bobbed my head and chuckled at the bleak diagnosis. "Episodes....yeah."

"Does your body fire a warning shot at all? Do you feel it coming?"

"Um . . . yeah, kinda. I mean..." Now I was rocking back and forth too. "I mean . . . my breath gets short . . . shallow. My tongue swells up, I think."

"OK, GOOD!" Jim pointed his index finger at me with excitement. "So when you just begin to feel any of that, OK, at the first sign, I want you to sit down and write. Write until the feeling's gone." He turned to Joe, who was sitting in meditative stillness "She's gonna need your support on that. When she goes to write, just let her go, OK? Get the kids, get the dinner, whatever. This is gonna be for your good, too. OK, dude?"

He was obviously looking to Joe for a committing gesture. A nod, fist bump, anything. Joseph, however, seemed to be checking out of the conversation, staring out the windows at the moon. This all in and then all out pattern made me nervous. Apparently Jim picked up on that, too.

"Joe, dude. She's doing this for you too, bro."

"Huh, what?" Joe shook his head as if he were bringing himself back from wherever his mind had wandered, "Yes. She can write. As much as she wants and prayer on Wednesdays at Reba's and church on Sunday. Got it."

Wow, I thought. That Marine can sure report. And maybe he does have my back.

After work the next day, I shuffled through our creaking lead glass and painted oak door, arms full of paperwork, newspaper, a water bottle and coffee mug. More than the heap in my arms was out of balance. My breath became short in my chest. My lips got numb, my head light.

It was time to write.

"Hi honey," I said as I planted a peck on Joe's prickly face. "I'm gonna go ahead and write real quick."

"Take your time," he said—in his most soothing baritone. "I've got the kids. I'll cook dinner."

"That's dreamy, baby," I said, "but I've got dinner planned. I'm just going to write for a bit."

Look at us, both doing what we promised.

Joe gave me the kind of a tap a coach gives a quarterback as he heads onto the field to get killed and with that, I stole away to our bedroom, laptop in hand, and closed the door.

Here is that first entry:
Tuesday, March 16, 2010
Day 1
4:01pm
I'm writing now because I can feel the shortness of breath sneaking in.
I'm feeling stressed, over-whelmed, a clenching in my jaw. I am biting my lip.
I'm a little dizzy.
It's tornado season.

It will be 11 years in April. April 9th to be exact. Shoot. 4:05 a.m. April 9th of 1999 in Montgomery, Ohio. To be exact.

7575 Cornell Road, Montgomery, Ohio, to be exact.

The home of Lee and Jacque Cook – my parents to be exact – was struck by a tornado and killed them both.

Not quite instantly – to be sadly and painfully exact – it cracked my father's skull wide open and crushed every bone in my mother's body to the point that the first neighbor to rush to her said, "She had no bones left."

My heart is beating hard in my chest. I can't exactly breathe. I'm gonna stop for a second and take three deep breaths and invite the Lord into my broken blown in heart.

OK.

In those breaths, I heard the Lord say "Good, Shannyn," and my pain moved from a level 9 or 10 to about a 3.

I'm writing this because I've made the decision to heal this year.

Every year, when the spring comes and the snow begins to thaw, I begin to panic sometimes and break down sometimes. This season, this spring, when I begin to panic – I'm going to run to the keyboard and write it all down. I'm gonna run to God.

I broke down for the first time this year on Saturday night at a friend's house.

I thought I was healed enough to hang with a girl and her mom. I guess I was wrong and so I've declared war on my brokenness.

My Plan.

1-Journal. Journal every stinking time I can't breathe, function, cope. When I'm breaking down I'm going to journal. I'm doing it every single day. Even on the good days to recount the progress and the Lord's goodness in my healing and in my pain.

2-Pray. I attend a small group on Wednesdays and Church on Sundays and I've spoken with my pastor. I'm getting all prayed up in whatever I feel I need prayer for and whatever my prayer partners feel led to pray for.

That's it.

That's my healing strategy.

I don't want another spring to go by and make me feel like I've been hit by a train or like I'm being hunted by a pack of dogs.

If that kind of brokenness is what the Lord needs to use me for his glory then I submit to His will but I am going to work hard to get my springtime back.

And then a few days later came this entry:

Yesterday at church, my pastor was teaching on honoring your Mother and Father.

I totally lost it in the back row and wept and wept and wept silently. I've gotten good at silent weeping, but a wonderful older couple in our church, Tom and Mary Quinlan noticed. They came to me and laid hands on me and spoke healing into my brokenness.

I said, "I still feel like I've been hit in the chest with a cannon ball."

Mary said, "What do you want to ask the Lord to DO with it?" "I want Him to take it away." I eked out. "I've asked Him a million times, already, Mary. I have." "Have you asked the Lord to FILL it?" she inquired. I shook my head 'no'. "Why don't we ask the Lord to fill it?" and we prayed that simple prayer. Lord, please send your Spirit and fill Shannyn's empty spot. Thank, Lord." "Amen," I said.

Taking my hands in hers, she whispered in my ear, "Psalm 103

Bless the Lord, O my soul, and all that is within me, bless His holy name."

That includes the tornado, my parent's death and the ruined shell of a girl that was left behind. Me.

I believe you; please help my disbelief (Mathew)

God, send your Spirit of healing to me and to all the broken and lost and fill our brokenness by your power.

Meet me here.

Touch my inmost being.

I love you, Father and even though I don't understand You, I trust you and all of my hope is in you.

Thank you for giving me the courage to walk through this valley of darkness and in the shadow of death.

I know that you are with me. Send me comfort.

In the name of the healer Jesus, I ask.

I carved out time to write after work each day at 4pm as the kids were home from school and having their time to unwind, with an after school box of crackers, a juice box and a noisy cartoon. It was also the time of day I usually unraveled a little, at least inside my head.

It was never as bad as when that voice would scream in my head, though. Thankfully that scream stopped one day while at a yoga workshop. I was moving through the postures and listening to the scream, like a soundtrack, when I suddenly realized that the scream was *me*! It has been my scream all along. "You go ahead and scream," I said to the voice in my head, "I'll just be here to listen. You don't have to stop. I'm here for you" and with that, the scream disappeared, never to return.

However the panic was still easy to find. It was, in fact, barely hidden.

I'd grab the laptop and head into my little lead glass front porch and follow Jim's simple recipe.

That was Part 1 of the Plan.

Part 2 began that first Wednesday when I got prayer from Rebecca.

She shut her bedroom door and sat beside me on her bed. "Lord," she said simply with her now comforting up-talk, "I just want to thank you for Joe and Shannyn and what you're doing in their family. God, we do pray for this broken, empty feeling that Shannyn has. Father, clothe her with your joy. Give her a garment of praise for her heaviness. In Jesus name. Amen."

It was a simple prayer. An everyday prayer. There was not a need for bells and whistles. No special effects required. We just said, "Hey,

God. We need your help here. Thanks." Not every great prayer requires 3D glasses.

On Day 9, Sunday after church, I was the crying girl, AGAIN! No big surprise there, right? As the prayer team came forward, Joseph ducked out to get a coffee and pick up Liam from kids' church. Joe normally wanted to jet the second church ended, but I was so thankful that he was happily upholding his end of the bargain and making room for the healing season in his schedule.

I went forward to get prayer *again* from the most angelic couple you will meet this side of heaven. Tom and Mary Quinlan were there at the front of the church, with their prayer badges on.

"We are so thankful to pray for you," Mary said. Her voice was soft as a pussy willow, her eyes the brightest of blues. "Tom was saying during church he'd like to pray for you. We saw you crying."

I'd been sobbing in absolute silence the entire time. I didn't think anyone but Joseph knew. I had tried to keep my shoulders so steady. I thought seriously someone should get this lady a Glinda the Good Witch bubble to float around in. She was just that cool. She should have wings, at least...and a crown.

"What's going on, Shannyn? How can we pray?" Tom said with his slightly Southern drawl.

I tried to talk and found I couldn't except to say, "My heart. It's broken. Same 'ol, same 'ol."

"I'm just going to pray over you in silence for a while, if that's OK." Tom looked like an old man version of Woody from Toy Story. I resisted the urge, even in my state to try to say, "Sure thing, partner." I couldn't if I wanted to.

Tom extended his hand over my head. I could feel warmth streaming from it into the top of my head. That's too hot to be just his hand, I thought. Or maybe he just has hot hands.

"Do you know why your heart is broken, honey?" Mary asked with a frosty-pink smile.

I nodded and cried a cry which had suddenly and awkwardly added sound. Loud, weeping sound at that. "I know," I heaved, "I know. It's cuz my mom and dad are dead and I MISS THEM SO MUCH!"

I was a total dumped-at-the altar wreck. Tom was praying out loud now. "Jesus, Jesus, come, Lord" he said. His words wiped the sweat from my brow.

"It...hurts..." I cried. "It hurts so much...oh Mary." I buried my face in her shoulder, still sobbing, and the smell of her perfume made me think of my mom, made me wish they could have met.

"Can you tell me *where* it hurts?" she asked, quietly, the way Mr. Rogers did.

"It's right here," I said. I made a giant circle with my hands and covered my gut with it. "It's a giant, gaping, aching empty spot, Mary, and I've asked the Lord a million times to take it away but it's still there –ere – ere. We asked Him to fill it? Remember?" My sobs were now echoes of themselves.

I raised my face to look at hers. In that instant, I'm sure my eyes caught a twinkle from theirs and started to sparkle, too.

"Let's ask Him to fill it again. We are not going to stop asking Daddy."

I shook my head 'yes.' Mary and Tom both laid their hands on me, Tom on my quivering head and Mary on my shaking shoulders. And they prayed heaven down.

"Lord, Jesus. Come into this place. Father, have your way," Mary implored of the heavenlies. "Father, we just ask you to fill this space in Shannyn's belly, Lord."

"Yes Lord, yes Lord." Tom was rocking on his feet like Jim did in his chair.

"God, as big as this space can be, Father we know that *you are bigger*, Lord. Fuller, deeper, wider, Father."

"Yes, Lord. Yes, Lord."

"Father fill her emptiness with tender…"

I was now rocking myself, but side to side like I was holding a restless baby.

"Yes, Lord."

"Warming, Father…"

"Mmmm…..yes…yes…Father"

"All-sustaining love, Lord."

We sat in the peace that the presence of the Holy Spirit brings, waiting, listening, soaking. As Tom finally lifted his hand from atop my bowed head, I breathed in deep and let it out slow. Peeking my eyes open to see their kind faces, I was surprised people were still milling around the school gym sanctuary. A little girl in a pink flower dress reached high to her daddy. "Uppie, Daddy," she said. I understood. I wanted to reach up high to our Father in heaven and have Him scoop me up, too. I had felt like we'd been there for days, at least hours, but apparently it was just a minute or two. I wiped my eyes and gave Tom and Mary a smile.

"How are you doing, Shannyn?" Tom asked.

"Good," I said, half surprised I could speak at all and *fully* surprised it was true. "I'm GOOD!"

What was this peace? I no longer wept. I was calm. And the vacuum that just moments earlier was camping out in my solar plexus like a squatting junkie in a ghetto house . . . was gone.

"How is that empty spot, honey? Do you feel any fullness?" Mary asked.

"Mary," I whispered, "it's gone."

"Oh, praise you Father! Thank you, Jesus." Tom was still quiet and rocking. His praises blew coolness on the beads of sweat still forming on my brow. "Praise you, Lord. Praise you, Abba Father, you are so good, God," he whispered.

"Yes, yes, holy holy," Mary sounded like she was blowing bubbles on a child's party. Each prayer and praise floated in rainbows of wonder up – up—up and POP! "In Jesus name. Amen."

They raised their hands from my head and shoulders and we had a giant group hug at the altar: Me, Tom and Mary and Jesus.

CHAPTER 12

WHY IT MATTERS

God, you amaze me. Thank you for the healing you're sending.
I pray this healing becomes a well-established part of who I am, allowing
me to be a compassionate help mate to everyone around me in your
name and for your glory.

I've seen the Lord heal a few times in my life. It never comes like I
expect. I've not yet seen it come in a flash or with a blaze of glory
or even in a mighty wind. I've never heard angels singing at the moment (although I knew they were) or felt the earth move under my
foot. For me, it comes softly.

Unnoticed. Under the radar.

In fact, I must need a better radar, because the Lord did in fact
fill my empty, broken place with his love and peace, just as His daughter had asked Him to that second time when Tom and Mary prayed.

It was subtle.

I just got my prayer and went on my merry way to head home to
fill up my crockpot with Sunday dinner. But when it came time to sit
down the next day and write about the pain, the grief, the brokenness,

the gaping wound, the empty spot…it was gone. Perched on the edge of my chair, laptop on TV tray, looking out the lead glass panels I scanned my body up and down. Where is the empty spot? I thought. Where *is* it? Had it moved? Had it shrunk so small it's hard to find?

I quieted myself, focused on my breath, asked God to give me insight as to where that empty spot was hiding. Then I dove in more deeply to see if I could find it. Even if the often cannon ball sized pain was now a tiny speck of sand-sized emptiness, I still wanted it full. I wanted a total healing and restoration because little pains hurt, too. Ever have a tiny rock in your shoe? It hurts, it hinders. It's like that with grief as well. Plus, I wanted total healing because that's what Jesus said He came to give me. That's what I was looking for and, dear one, that's exactly what I got.

There was no hidden speck of emptiness. It was not there. For the first time I could remember, I was full. I was restored by the unfailing grace of the living God. (Christianese, but it's true) He'd done it!

Now, you'd think my next stop would have been to get on the radio and shout victory, but I kept it to myself, not even telling Joseph at first.

Although I knew in my heart that I had been restored, I did not announce it anywhere. I didn't post a blog that day shouting *healing* from the mountain top or rejoice with my small group that day. I was afraid that it might only be a temporary reprieve and I didn't want to discredit the King, should my pain return, in the same way as someone who is in a 12-step-progam remains anonymous…so as not to discredit the program should they fall.

In fact the next day I simply took my newly healed heart out on a spin to a yoga workshop, although not just any workshop, a workshop with John Friend, my favorite yoga teacher. He is the founder and originator of the style of yoga that I used to love the most, Anusara. It means 'flowing with grace' in Sanskrit.

This is the healing season blog entry from that day:

Day 11

Anusara is all about opening the heart.

The workshop was amazing and at this point, when I check in with my heart, I feel no pain, no brokenness, no void, and no emptiness. I feel full of grace. AMAZING grace!

However, my hamstrings are another story.

The one thing that bothered me at the workshop was the lack of Jesus being represented. John acknowledged many so-called deities, but never the Most High. Strange.

Also in the workshop, was a Christian pastor from Grand Rapids, Michigan, and he and I talked and decided that we would be prayer partners, praying that the Lord would send His Holy Spirit to open the eyes of John's (the teacher's) heart to the vast truth of gospel. We would pray that JOHN would open to God's grace. Here are some things that I know from the yogic practice that I believe are directly related to my heart's peace today.

First-Open to grace. In my framework-that means open to the expansive healing power of your Father in heaven who loves you and longs for your wholeness in Him.

Second-Engage. Hug to the middle. In yoga this means drawing your muscles to the bone. It means participating and not just having a "whatever" attitude to how your heart and your life are going. You have a vote. In my Christian framework, this means, Hug to Christ, who is the center of absolutely everything.

Third-Shine out. Make this movement an offering. In my Christian framework, this means pray and shine His light with everything you do. Let your light shine before men so that people will see your good works and give credit to your Father. I noticed John took a lot of credit.

Another helpful thing to remember is to keep your shoulders on your back. Try it.

Bring your shoulders forward and feel how you heart closes. Now draw them onto you back and see how the horizon of your heart expands. This simple act has kept deep depression at bay for me some days. Sometimes it's scary

because it means being open and vulnerable, which means we could get hurt –
but if I can't trust opening to grace, then I am straight-up sunk.

Prayer:

Father, I thank you that I had the chance to share Jesus with so many
people today. I pray that I will always have the chance to share the good news
and that I will always have the courage to do it when you guide me to.

Thank you that today my heart doesn't feel pain. I am open to the idea
that I can live each day this way. I sure did love not feeling blown up today,
God. Thank you. Will you please help it stick? Will you teach me how to honor
the memory of Mom and Dad without grieving them? You are amazing, Lord,
and all of my hope and trust is in you.

Thanks for being trust-worthy.

I offer my joyful heart to you with gratitude.

Amen.

Scripture:

Let the peace of God rule in your hearts. Colossians 3:15 NIV

I was less than two weeks into that 40 day challenge at the time
the Lord healed my heart for good, but I'd committed to Jim and
to myself to continue for the healing season...until Mother's Day. I
knew, as well, that even if God had filled in that space for good and
it wasn't just a conjugal visit with my own peace, the days ahead were
likely to be filled with hidden minefields.

My birthday was coming . . . always a trigger to my sorrow.

Robin's eggs . . . trigger.

Crocus bursting from the ground with their victorious hopeful
cry...trigger.

Easter . . . the time we celebrate any hope in this life at all . . . the
empty tomb, people! Victory! Freedom! And a giant . . . trigger.

On and on it would go . . . or could go if I did not work to bring
His healing to those places, and so, on and on I wrote.

And just days later, I'd write the following:

"I did the math. The anniversary of the tornado is April 9th. Today is March 30th and the Lord healed my heart 10 days ago. That means for 3,996 days, I lived with an utterly blown-up, exploded, pulverized mess of a broken heart. If you include the fact that it was already broken at the time the tornado that killed both my parents hit, I was a broken and beat up mess for 4,511 days, and as of now, I've been healed for 10."

You may recognize that entry, because it is how this book began. He did it. He did it! God healed me, friend. If as you read this, you are scanning your body and are keenly aware of your empty-broken spot, then Jesus can fill you up, too.

The scream I always heard in my head quieted. The roller coaster of running to my yoga class to find peace just to watch it slip away before the day was done, no longer a cycle. The short breath, the numb lips, the shaking hands that dropped dishes (and threw dishes), He healed them.

The anger and resentment over what I perceived as a less than perfect upbringing had been exchanged for mercy and forgiveness.

And remember when I told Alex, "Mommy's OK, but she may cry forever?" Well, I don't. I. Do. Not. What's more, I have joy and I sincerely pray that gives you hope. It is only by His grace. Time does not heal all wounds. That's a myth. But God? That's another story.

Now, when the snow starts to melt, I look forward to getting back in my garden instead of starting to panic. When Mother's Day comes, I can celebrate the important women in my life, enjoy my family blessing me and even feel grateful that my friends have their moms to honor instead of feeling heartbreak and resentment.

And since my healing, nothing has ever been the same in our marriage. We have peace between us. Deep peace.

Joe and I began to feel a spiritual unity that we never had before we both were saved. We have the same rule book, the Bible. We now know how to resolve problems by opening the Bible and doing what it says, even if we don't *like* it. It always works. Yes, we still do have problems, sometimes big ones, but it is nothing like before. God lives in us. We honor the Christ in each other in an entirely new and holistic, in fact holy, way. Glory of the Father, to the praise of the Son through the power of the Holy Spirit. And that foolproof God-plan I talked about earlier? That plan is working to this day, as we both continue to practice loving each other. God has redeemed us. He has healed us.

The wounds from Joseph's rage are redeemed and forgiven.

The agonies of dashed expectations are replaced with gratitude.

I'm not talking about a pair of rose colored glasses. I'm talking about two sinful, broken people who have chosen God's way and as a result enjoy a thriving and stable marriage for ourselves and for our children.

This simple commitment (1) to recognize that I was in fact triggered by this change in seasons (2) to admit that my brokenness was hurting other people and (3) to commit to a 40 day healing season cleared the debris of a lifetime of missed steps, disappointments, disaster and wreckage. And it was simple.

By carving out time each day to breathe, write and pray and by allowing my brothers and sisters in Christ to intervene with prayer only two times a week, I was restored, made whole again, set free and, as we know, the one the Son sets free is free indeed.

I can look back with that same grace on my ex-husband, John. In light of God's amazing forgiveness, how can I hang onto the regret of a failed marriage, especially as I stand witness to the miracle that God did in and through Joseph David Caldwell?

My relationship with myself is in right order for the first time ever. I am not the center of my universe any more, and neither is Joseph. Jesus is the center of my universe, which works much better. Obviously, as Jesus *is* the center of the universe, after all.

Now we serve a God who is not out there somewhere. He is here. He is now. The great I Am...is. I don't worship the universe. I worship the one who made the universe and came into the mess that we made and lived out His beautiful plan and set it straight.

I am forgiven. I am loved. I am forgiving and loving. He's not mad at me anymore. I'm not mad at me anymore. I'm not mad. I am clothed in grace and hidden in Christ. That's why it's called saved.

How did God do it?

Did he use people?

Yes! I'm so glad, so grateful that Jim and Meg and Reba and Lorna and LaJeana and Laura, Lori the Quinlan's and Noreen and the many others from the church did not look at our mess and thumb their noses at it or gossip, "Look at the awful things that happen to a family when they do not walk with Jesus. Look at the Caldwell's and learn, children. Do not play at their house."

In fact, it was the opposite. They, like the firefighters on 9-11, ran into the fire and extinguished it with living water. They walked Him to me. Our family could have been a sermon illustration either way. It could be a story about how your life crashes when you do not do what the Bible says; we were surely a case study in that. But the sermon that was written was about how Jesus came for the sick and how He still wants to be at the table with them...with me and you.

He used the Bible, its study and standing on His Word.

Did he use worship? Yes!

Did he use prayer and writing?

Yes and yes!

Did He use yoga? For me...yes, He surely did. Yoga, you may not know, is a Sanskrit word which means "union" and it is so called because of the link between the breath and movement, and man and his Creator. You may be waiting for me to completely denounce my yogic past and say it was a sinful lie. I'm not going to say that, because for me it was an imperative piece of the healing God gave me. I found Him there. It's from that language that I had a frame of reference for *be still and know that I am God*. Obviously, if you feel God is convicting you about practicing...don't. Otherwise, if you are in your healing season, a Christian yoga class may be a very good idea. If that makes you uncomfortable, look to you Bibles and do what it says or ask your pastor to talk with you about it. Pray on it. See what God gives you.

I can tell you this for sure, though: it's a good thing that my hope was not in yoga, or in my favorite discipline of yoga, Anusara or in its founder, John Friend. It's a good thing that I did not follow John (as many did), but rather followed Jesus or my heart may have burst again just weeks after that wonderful heart-opening workshop as John Friend had to step down as head of the organization he founded in the wake of a gruesome and ugly scandal. How great is it that God put me and Pastor Andre on our yoga mats and in John Friend's face to show him the cross of Jesus around our necks and to pray, pray, pray for the Lord to move in John's heart? Perhaps John will find Jesus, too. I pray he does, so he can know what it really means to open to grace and find real, full freedom and forgiveness.

For myself, I am up to my elbows in forgiveness and each day He gives me breath and life to walk on His earth. I live to praise Him.

Sometimes healing comes through humbly forgiving Joseph, as he so often forgives me.

Sometimes it's on the air doing my morning show on Family Life Radio, just lifting His name.

Sometimes it's on my blog as I tap tap tap the keyboard to share this hope.

Sometimes it's in my garden, as I pick veggies and remember how abundant and extravagant He surely is.

Sometime it's in dancing with children. Sometimes it's feeding the homeless...or just smiling and praying with them.

Sometimes I praise Him with song and now, when I go to church and the worship band breaks out with "You are so good to me! You heal my broken heart. You are my Father in heaven!" I sing along to *every* word.

Why did God heal me so completely?

Well, that's an easier one. He did it for love. He did it for mercy. He did it because it gives Him glory to set us free. Because it's who He is. Because it's what He does. It's how He rolls.

He did it to give me a purpose, a purpose that I admit rang hollow to me even after I read the first saving lines of that wonderful Rick Warren book. My purpose, which no longer feels empty or saccharine, is to make Him known, to make him famous. It's to give hope away.

There is good news. Great news as we read in Luke, *shall be for all man (and woman) kind. Unto us is born a Savior, Christ . . . the Lord.*

He is relentless in His loving and kind pursuit of his children...all of us, not just me. Not just my church lady friends, everyone.

I want other people who suffer as I did to know that Jesus swears He will not leave us. He's not like husbands who walk out in the night. He's not like bosses who fire us for cybershopping from our desktops. He's not a condemning father, quick to point out our failures without offering to help. He steps down from heaven to kneel down beside us and show us how it's done. He knows we can't do it so He intervenes. He did for me, through His people, through His Spirit and through his living Word! Surely God is with us!

Want even more good news? Great! Check this! Even when He stoops by our side to show us how it's done and we look with our giant baby eyes at him and nod our heads and swear to do it right next time, just to turn around and mess it all up again...He still loves us, heals us, forgives us and works with us time and time and time again to set things right. He will not stop and He is not stoppable.

My purpose is to let everyone know that He's mighty to save – everything. For you who have just taken my journey with me, thank you. Everything I leave in these pages is for you and for your healing.

This book exists not just to tell you about the great and glorious things that God has done in my life. It is to give you the real hope that He wants to do it in your life, too. He wants to bring healing to *us*. That's His total M.O.

This simple method, *The Healing Season*, is yours.

If you've got a tornado (or tornados) which pick at your emotional scabs and leave you wounded, this is for you. If you choose to embark on your own healing season, I suggest that you choose a time to get with God and your breath and a way to write it out at the time of day you are least likely to be distracted and put it on your schedule as non-negotiable. You owe it to yourself and your loved ones to really, really go for it – and that means no distractions.

I know it's a tall order, especially if you are a mom or dad, but it's OK. Just explain to whoever you need to that you will be working on being a better, more whole you and part of that is a little quiet for 40 days. Ask your loved ones to give their blessing and then hold yourself and them to it. You will be amazed by how the Lord will bless that.

I sincerely pray that this gives you help and hope for whatever it is that you are walking through and the courage to work for your peace.

Where you need freedom, I pray you'll find it.

Where you're holding back or holding on, I pray you'll let go and let God.

Where you're trying to fake your way, as I did, through your life, why not take a risk and hold fast to the truth and cast your cares on Him, for He says He cares for you? Why not bring it to the One who knows the truth and *is* the truth?

Where are you settling for just enough instead of everything? Why not believe God on His extravagant promises? Is it easy, this journey you'll embark on? No...not always, but neither was the cross. Is it good? Yes. Yes, indeed.

You can bet your life on it.

If you are ready to begin your *Healing Season,* I offer this first step: Give your life to Jesus. He is real, alive and is the Healer. This is the prayer that Joseph prayed that day with Pastor Jim, a bit of Joseph's letter to me and a bit of Mary Quinlan's prayer thrown in for good measure. If you need Jesus (and we all do) take a moment to pray this, either with a friend or alone with your Lord. That is how your healing season begins.

Lord, Jesus

I am so sorry for the many times I fail.

God, I'm trying my best and I still fall so short.

The only reason I can think of for my failure, is that I'm broken.

The only solution for my brokenness I can think of is you, Jesus.

I believe your death and resurrection are big enough to cover me.

Come into my heart, Lord

I give myself to you right now.

Teach me how to live and how to love.

Fill up my broken and empty spots by the power of your Holy Spirit, now alive in me.

Thank you for saving me.

Use my story for your glory.

In Jesus' name.

I (name) prayed this prayer on (date)

ORDERING INFORMATION

The Healing Season by Shannyn Caldwell
is available on Amazon and Kindle.

For information on

Healing Season Workshops, other resources

or

to invite Shannyn to speak at your event

go to

www.ShannynCaldwell.com

10808649R00144

Made in the USA
San Bernardino, CA
28 April 2014